WHAT MOTHER TERESA TAUGHT ME

D0108950

WHAT MOTHER TERESA TAUGHT ME

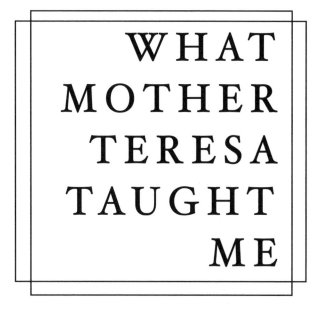

MARYANNE RAPHAEL

ST. ANTHONY MESSENGER PRESS
Cincinnati, Ohio

Scripture passages have been taken from *New Revised Standard Version Bible,*
copyright ©1989 by the Division of Christian Education of the National Council
of the Churches of Christ in the U.S.A., and used by permission. All rights reserved.

Cover and book design by Mark Sullivan
Cover image © Kapoor Balder/Sygma/CORBIS

LIBRARY OF CONGRESS CATALOGING-IN-PUBLICATION DATA

Raphael, Maryanne.
What Mother Teresa taught me / Maryanne Raphael.
p. cm.
Includes bibliographical references.
ISBN 978-0-86716-810-5 (pbk. : alk. paper) 1. Teresa, Mother, 1910-1997. 2.
Missionaries of Charity–Biography. 3. Nuns–India–Calcutta–Biography. 4.
Christian life–Catholic authors. 5. Spiritual life–Catholic Church. I. Title.

BX4406.5.Z8R38 2007
271'.97–dc22
[B]
2007029131

ISBN 978-0-86716-810-5

Published by St. Anthony Messenger Press
28 W. Liberty St.
Cincinnati, OH 45202
www.AmericanCatholic.org

Printed in the United States of America.
Printed on acid-free paper.

07 08 09 10 11 5 4 3 2 1

Contents

Acknowledgments

I WISH TO THANK MOTHER TERESA FOR THE LETTER OF PERMISSION THAT allowed me access to her Missionaries of Charity, Coworkers and friends. I thank all of them for their willing cooperation: Jacqueline de Decker, International Link of the Sick and Suffering Coworkers; Ann Blaikie, International Link of the Coworkers; Vi Collins, National Link of the Coworkers; Michael and Agnes Gomes, Mother Teresa's friends and first landlords in whose "upper room" she began the Missionaries of Charity; Ed and Dorothy Baroch, Youth Link of the Coworkers of Mother Teresa; Dr. Anita Figueredo, Mother's friend and longtime Coworker; Lillian Miceli-Farrugia, International Youth Link; the Missionaries of Charity and the many Coworkers who helped: Irene Nicolai, Karis Chodzko, Phyllis Cooper, Salud Rodriquez, Zulema Hokanson, Grace Kessler, Lupe Rios, Nancy Morgan, Susanna Miranda and Phyllis Cooper; and Margaret Delaney.

Marcella Roth, Ann Liddell, J.R. Roosenberg, Tom Patterson, Tom White, Susie Chesser, Doris Nocera, Kathy Hamilton, Shannon Brady, Dr. Eve Jones, Karen Marie Kitterman and Bonnie Monahan.

Don Johnson, who kept my computer working.

Mary Sue Seymour, my literary agent, and Lisa Biedenbach, my editor.

All who read this book.

And I wish to thank my family, especially my son Raphael, who at the age of two shared Mother's faith in prayer. Whenever we passed a place of worship, he insisted on entering "to say hello to God." I'd say, "We're late for your doctor. Let's see him first and then say hello to God." Although he was usually obedient, he would insist we stop. "We'll say a prayer and ask God to get us to the doctor on time." So we stopped for a few minutes, and God always got us there on time.

—Maryanne Raphael

Foreword

Maryanne Raphael's book about Mother Teresa and the Missionaries of Charity is an accurate, clearly written biography that all will find inspiring and instructive. It manages to convey the spirit of Mother and the Missionaries of Charity in a manner that all who know them will recognize as authentic and all who have not had that privilege will want to become acquainted with and learn from them.

The book is easy to read and very informative. I recommend it to all readers, especially young ones, whether they have been devoted followers of Mother Teresa or have not known her except as a person often written about by the press. All will find inspiration in it. *What Mother Teresa Taught Me* is a work of love by the author, and it shows.

–Anita Figueredo, M.D.,
*Member of the Board of Trustees
of the University of San Diego,
Coworker and longtime friend
of Mother Teresa*

Introduction

SPENDING TIME WITH MOTHER TERESA AND HER MISSIONARIES OF
Charity enriched my life, and I want to share Mother's warm spirit,
wisdom and unconditional love. Mother said, "If God calls you into
the street, go into the street with a smile, but don't go unless he calls
you. If he calls you into a palace, go there with a smile."

She taught me to stop worrying and to trust God. She helped
me to see my would-be enemy as Jesus in his most distressing disguise. She said, "A smile is the beginning of peace."

Mother Teresa gave you her complete attention and affection.
She looked at you and saw God. And when you walked away you carried some of her love and joy inside. I hope you feel Mother's spirit
as you read this.

When Mother Teresa gave me permission to write about the
Missionaries of Charity and her work, she said, "Pray that your
book glorifies God and brings many souls to him."

So please help me pray.

Part One

MOTHER TERESA'S LIFE AND WORK

"Do small things with great love."
–Mother Teresa

1

S K O P J E

At the turn of the twentieth century, Agnes Bojaxhiu's parents, two young Albanians, very much in love, married in the town of Prizen in Serbia. Dranafile ("Drana") Bernai was gentle but strong, while Nikola was a handsome young man working for an independent Albania. Although most Albanians were Muslims or Orthodox Jews, both Drana and Nikola came from generations of devout Roman Catholics.

After their wedding Drana and Nikola settled in Skopje, Macedonia, a small mountain town in the Turkish Ottoman Empire where East met West, where Muslims, Christians and Jews lived together in relative peace. Nikola and an Italian friend had a successful construction business. Soon Nikola owned several houses and joined Skopje's town council.

A daughter, Aga, was born in 1905, and three years later a son, Lazar, named for Nikola's father. Then two daughters died shortly after birth. Finally on August 26, 1910, baby Agnes Gonxha was born. She had round cheeks and sparkling eyes, and one day would be Mother Teresa of Calcutta, founder of the Missionaries of Charity, and Nobel Peace Prize winner.

Although a mischievous tomboy, from an early age Agnes was devoted to her family and to her church.

One hot afternoon in 1919, nine-year-old Agnes skipped along a cobblestone street in Skopje's business district peering into shop windows. She watched the shepherds grazing their sheep on the nearby mountains. She passed the gypsy quarter, smiling at the peasants in their homespun black tops and baggy, brightly colored pantaloons. Agnes's whole world was Skopje, a beautiful rugged mountain village dominated by a huge mosque and a sixteenth-century Byzantine fortress.

Nearing her home, she heard laughter and hastened to join the fun. Her fourteen-year-old sister, Aga, and her eleven-year-old brother, Lazar, sat on the sofa whispering jokes and giggling. Agnes greeted her mother who sat in a rocking chair darning socks. Drana glanced first at Agnes, then at the clock on the wall.

Agnes soon had her brother collapsing on the living room rug. Drana tried to ignore the steadily rising crescendo. Quickly and without a change of expression, she stood up, lay her sewing on the table and left the room. Suddenly the entire house went dark. The laughter stopped.

"What happened?" the children asked.

"There is no need to waste light on such foolishness," their mother's voice cut through the darkness. "Idleness is a sin. Now I am sure you children can find something constructive to do."

She threw the main switch and the subdued children did their tasks when the lights reappeared. Their mother again glanced at the clock and rushed to change her dress and brush her hair. She returned to the living room just as her husband entered the house. He kissed her.

"You look tired," she said. "How was your meeting?"

"Intense," he sighed. "Everyone knows Kosovo is part of Albania. The province is full of Albanians. Why can't the people decide what country they belong to?"

Drana gently wiped his face with a large white handkerchief.

"We must pray about it. But first come and have some moscht."

"Father!" the three children greeted Nikola. As they competed for his attention, he laughed and covered his ears. "I have two ears, but I can only hear one of you at a time."

Later the family knelt in the living room before the Blessed Mother's statue as Drana led them in the rosary. "And Blessed Mother, please ask your Son to bless Kosovo and Skopje, Albania, and everywhere on earth."

"Amen."

The next evening the children sat at the top of the stairs listening to Nikola's friends discussing the political situation. Agnes loved her attractive father with his dark hair and eyes, muscular build and energetic walk. She also liked his friends, but their intensity frightened her as they tried to out-shout each other. When their voices grew louder, the children became apprehensive. Nikola exploded, "Kosovo must be free."

Hours later, Drana told her husband, "I wish you didn't have to go to Belgrade."

"Drana, you know this dinner is important. We are winning important allies."

She nodded her head, shut her eyes and held him close.

Nikola returned from Belgrade late the following evening. He walked woodenly into the house. Drana rose to welcome him but stopped puzzled as he wove his way across the room.

He began coughing up blood. She cried, "Nikola!" The children came running and watched in silence as their mother knelt over Nikola's crumpled body.

"Agnes," Drana said, "run to Sacred Heart for a priest!"

The child realized her beloved father was near death. She slipped out of her nightgown and into her uniform. Agnes had never before left the house alone after dark. The church was on the same street, only a block and a half away, but her heart beat rapidly as she ran, pushing herself to run faster. She had to see that her father received the last sacraments.

She pounded on the rectory door. "Please, God, help us!" The housekeeper opened the door and said, "I'm sorry, child. Father is out of town until late tonight."

Agnes ran to the railway station. "You've got to help me, God!" The station was nearly deserted, but a tall, thin priest she had never seen before sat on a bench.

"Father!" she ran toward him. "My father is dying. Please come with me!" The priest ran with her to the house.

Nikola was barely alive. The priest gave him the last rites, but the dying man was so weak that he could hardly raise his head. He smiled briefly and spoke a few soft words. The priest blessed the family and left. Drana made arrangements to transport Nikola to the nearby hospital.

In the waiting room the family prayed. The hours ticked ominously by. The three children had never seen their father sick. They fought tears and huddled together.

Drana sat alone, her hands folded in her lap, praying silently for the best and steeling herself for the worst. She led her children into the familiar routine of their daily rosary.

Late that night, a weary doctor mopped his sweat-soaked brow. "I am sorry, Mrs. Bojaxhiu. We did all we could." The girls gasped.

Lazar, with clenched fists, leapt to his feet. His eyes were swollen, and he choked back tears. "Father was murdered because he was working for a free Kosovo!"

Aga buried her face in Drana's lap while Agnes cried uncontrollably. Drana wiped away her own tears and said, "It's hard to lose the people we love. But feeling sorry they died is selfish. Dying is going home to God. We know your Papa is in heaven with Our Lady and Jesus. Let us try to be happy for him." She had the children's undivided attention. "We have to keep our family together.

Remember God is our Father and he is taking care of us." Drana took the children home and tucked them into bed, something she had not done since they were little.

Before Nikola died, the family was fairly well-off financially. They lived in one of the two spacious houses they owned, and they had a lovely garden with flowers and fruit trees. After Nikola died, his business partner, Mr. Morten, came to the house. "The business is off a frightening percentage, Mrs. Bojaxhiu. I've had to let most of our employees go," he said while hoisting a teacup. He was a rotund individual with small, hard eyes. Drana felt ashamed of thinking that his girth suggested he had never missed a meal.

"But Nikola always said business was doing well."

"Nikola was a dreamer. He never paid attention to business. No, he gallivanted all over the country talking politics. If he had stayed out of politics, he would probably be alive today. I worked my fingers to the bone trying to save our accounts with little or no help."

"What exactly are you saying, Mr. Morten?"

He cleared his throat and placed his teacup in its saucer. "Madam," he began haltingly, "I've had to sell off all our holdings to pay our debts. It is going to cost me even my own personal savings."

"Are you saying there is no money?" Drana asked.

"I'm afraid it's true, Mrs. Bojaxhiu. The business has gone broke."

"But we are depending on the business."

"You have my deepest sympathy, Madam. But there is nothing I can do. My lawyer will contact you in a few days. Good afternoon."

Drana was on her knees praying when the children arrived home. She blurted out the news.

"How will we live without Father's business?" Lazar asked.

"God is always with us," Drana reminded them.

"There is something rotten in this, Mother," said Lazar. "Father's business was doing OK. They're stealing it from us."

"I know, child," she said. "But we are not experienced in business, and we can't prove it. God must have other plans for us."

Months later, passing the building that had held their father's business, the three children spotted the sign on the front door: CLOSED.

Drana had to sell the house next door and forfeit the rent, their sole income since Nikola's death. They sold furniture, valuable clocks and family heirlooms.

"Why did Papa have to die?" Lazar asked as their possessions were loaded on a cart.

"They are only objects," Drana said. "We still have each other."

"I will leave school and find work," Lazar said.

"God has blessed you children with excellent minds, and you insult him if you don't use them."

Drana prayed. "Blessed Mother, help me create a Nazareth where I can raise my little ones."

One day Aga remarked, "Our clothes are so tattered."

"I've been so preoccupied I've forgotten my sewing. That's it!" she said. "I can sell homemade clothes and embroidered rugs!"

She put up a sign: "Clothes For Sale." Her friends brought in more items for her to sell.

Agnes came home one afternoon to find Drana assisting an old woman. "My own family doesn't want me," the woman said.

"I'm glad you're home, Agnes," Drana said, easing the old woman onto the sofa. "I need you to help me prepare your room for our sick neighbor. She has a tumor and she is very ill. If we don't help her, she will die."

Agnes asked, "How can a family not want its grandmother because she is ill?" Drana stopped turning down the blanket and took her daughter's hands and whispered, "It is awful for a family to turn its back on someone when he or she is sick or in trouble, but human beings are weak and do fall into such sins. But Our Lord says we are not to judge anyone. You can move in with your sister for a while."

Drana finished preparing the bed then turned to her daughter. "Agnes, I don't tell you children nearly enough how much I appreciate you. The days are so busy. There just isn't time for hugging and kissing the way your father did."

"That's all right, Mother," Agnes said.

Some hours later Agnes was sitting on Aga's bed when Lazar entered the room, all excited. "I'm going to military school!" Agnes was shocked.

"Mother has given her permission, and I have a scholarship." With a big grin he watched for a sign of her approval.

"What's the matter?" he asked.

"You're going away?" she asked.

"Yes, Agnes, we've always talked about it."

"Yes," she said, "but I didn't think it would be so soon."

Aga entered the room and heard the gist of the discussion. "Congratulations, Lazar," she said. "Father would be so proud." Aga hugged her brother, and Lazar looked to Agnes, who finally followed suit.

"Don't worry," he said. "I'll be home before you know it, holidays and all."

The days before Lazar's departure whisked by swiftly, and one morning the family was at the train station bidding the young man good-bye. He embraced his mother and two sisters.

"First Papa, Now Lazar," Agnes said.

"Lazar's coming back," Aga said.

"The time will pass faster than you can imagine," Drana promised.

The days turned into months, and the old woman that Drana had taken in prospered after countless hot meals, warm baths, fervent prayers and kind words. Her health and her strength returned. One morning she was well enough to seek her own lodgings.

With Nikola's death and Lazar away at school, Drana, Aga and Agnes put their energy into their church activities. They attended daily Mass and people gathered in their home to pray, plan church festivals, practice religious plays and help those in need. Both Agnes and Aga joined the Catholic Sodality Movement dedicated to the Blessed Virgin Mary.

When Agnes was twelve, a Jesuit priest spoke of his work in India and changed her life. "Most Indians go to bed hungry every night. Many of them know nothing about Jesus. They feel that no one cares about them." Agnes had never imagined masses of people starving to death. On the walk home, Aga asked, "How can people live their whole lives on the street, always hungry, and hot or cold, thirsty and sick?"

"That's like asking why Jesus had to suffer and die on the cross. It's a mystery," Agnes said.

The priest had said, "Each person has to follow his own road." Agnes wondered what road God had chosen for her.

The First Calling

EVERYONE LOVED AGNES WITH HER RICH SENSE OF HUMOR. SHE WAS kind, considerate and compassionate. Like Aga, she was a soloist in the church choir with a lovely voice. Agnes's parents had always been proud of her. Feeling she would be a good wife and mother, they looked forward to grandchildren.

Lorenz Antoni, Agnes's second cousin, admired her intelligence, enthusiasm and creativity.

Agnes loved Lorenz's notes about music. He was the only one she shared her diary with. He understood what she wrote. She loved his sensitivity, his encouragement and his devotion to God.

Lorenz wrote music, played several instruments and had his own orchestra. He taught Agnes to play the mandolin.

Agnes was sometimes restless walking down the winding streets of Skopje, sitting quietly in the living room, kneeling in the flower garden or climbing the hills beyond the town. "What am I doing for Jesus? Am I ready to follow if he calls?"

She felt something missing in her soul that only God could fill. She thought of Joan of Arc and Saint Paul who were tortured and martyred for their faith. She longed to die for God. Then she was repulsed by the idea. But she always said, "Lord, I am yours. Do whatever you want with me." Then she felt at peace.

Six years after Agnes first heard a priest speaking of India, Father Jambrenkovic, her family's priest, spoke of India again. Agnes felt God calling her. "Yes, Lord," she whispered, "I'll follow you wherever you say."

She asked Lorenz, "How can I know if God is calling me?"

Lorenz said, "I remember Father saying that great joy is the sign of a vocation."

"I have felt such joy." Tears ran down her cheeks. "Oh, I feel joy, but it will be hard leaving Skopje. I may never see my mother again, or Aga, or Lazar, or you."

"I always thought we'd grow old together," said Lorenz. "Even after we both got married, we would stay best friends. We are cousins, and we have shared our diaries and our secret dreams."

"I will miss you," Agnes said.

"I will miss you, too," he said. "But, Agnes, will your mother let you go?"

"You know my mother," Agnes said. "She would never say no to Jesus." The next day Agnes told Father Jambrenkovic, "I believe God wants me to serve him in India."

The priest studied the young girl, then said, "I will recommend you to an order of Irish nuns who work in India."

"Oh, thank you, Father!"

When Agnes got home, her mother was bent over the sink cutting vegetables. Agnes stood behind her in silence. Then she said, "Mother, I feel God is calling me to be a missionary in India." Drana put down the potato she was paring, cleaned up the peelings, covered the pot and left the room without saying a word. Agnes watched her mother climb the stairs. She heard her mother's bedroom door close. She waited.

She prayed, "God, you called me to follow you. Surely you can help my mother. Please, don't let me cause her pain." Agnes slipped into her mother's chair. She stared at the evening sky and at the distant mountains, the hills of home. Were there hills in India? Of course, some of the world's highest mountains, the Himalayas. She wondered where in India she would go. She remembered how far from Skopje India was. She might never again see her village or her loving relatives and friends. Never again to see anyone she had known her entire life. No wonder her news upset her mother.

When she looked at the sky again, it was black. Stars shone everywhere. Still no sounds from her mother's room. Was she crying? Agnes had never seen her cry.

She was probably saying a rosary, asking God to let her know his will. Agnes began saying her own rosary. Even at age eighteen, she loved meditating on the scenes from Jesus' life as she recited the Ave Marias. Agnes was still saying her rosary when Aga touched her shoulder. She jumped. "What's wrong, Agnes? Where is mother? Hasn't she started dinner yet? It's almost seven. I thought I'd be late."

"Mother's in her room."

"Is she sick? Have you checked on her?" Aga started up the stairs.

"Wait, Aga!" Agnes called. "I think Mother wants to be alone. Come! Let's talk. You know I've always thought God might call me to be a missionary. I have prayed about it, and I spoke with Father Jambrenkovic. He feels I have a vocation. He told me to pray some more and to discuss it with Mother."

"And that's what is going on with Mother?" Aga asked. "What did you tell her?"

"What I told you."

"And what did she say?"

"Nothing. She went to her room hours ago." The two sisters finished cutting the vegetables and put them on to boil. When the food was ready, it was almost bedtime and their mother had not come downstairs.

Drana stayed in her room for twenty-four hours. It was late afternoon when she started down the stairs. Agnes tried to decipher her mother's complete lack of expression. "Dear Lord, please let my mother give her blessing."

"My little Gonxha," her mother said. "I wish I could keep you with me always, but I see that in your heart you have already left us." She took Agnes's hand. "Come, there is much to do before you leave."

"Thank you, Mother, for understanding," Agnes said.

"Just keep your hand in Jesus' hand," her mother said.

That year Albania had become a monarchy under King Zog I. And Lazar, having graduated from the military academy in Tirana, had been promoted to lieutenant. In a letter she told him she planned to become a nun. His reply shocked her. "How could a girl like you become a nun? Do you realize you are burying yourself?"

Agnes was disappointed. She wrote, "You think you are so important as an official serving the king of two million subjects. Well, I shall be serving the king of the whole world!"

When Agnes told Lorenz she was going to be a nun, he asked, "When are you leaving?"

"Next week," she said.

"You work fast," he smiled.

"It is God's work," she said. "He's my king now. He has always been my king, of course. Now it is official."

"We will miss you. Our lives will be less interesting without you. I'm glad we are cousins. There will be a link between us even when we are apart."

"God's love links all of us together," she said.

The young people of the church sodality and choir had a concert and dedicated the last section to Agnes as their farewell.

Before she left, Agnes went through her closet, preparing her clothes for the poor. Each dress brought its own memories and emotions. "What memories will I make in the future?" she wondered.

She would never again wear pretty dresses. Soon her entire wardrobe would consist of the Loreto nun's habit, a long black gown with long sleeves and a white collar. Her hair would be cut off and she would wear a veil. The change was becoming real, and part of her reached out eagerly for it, but the other part wondered just where she was headed. When she left the boxes at the church, she felt she was leaving part of herself. "Let it be the frivolous part of me," she thought.

She took a last look at the church and headed home. "Please, God, let me keep my love of laughter, learning and life. Even if I'm to dress somberly at all times, let me know the joy of my vocation."

Drana and Aga gave Agnes a going away party. Her friends brought gifts. Lorenz gave her a gold fountain pen. "Maybe you won't be a famous writer," he laughed, "but you can continue your diary. And once in a while I would like a letter."

It seemed to Agnes that she had hardly shut her eyes when Drana knocked on the door. A short time later Agnes, Drana and Aga were at the train station. Some students and some Sacred Heart parishioners came to say good-bye. Lorenz approached them. "Nephew, please get us three tickets to Zagreb," Drana said. (Drana and Aga were going with Agnes for the first part of the journey.) Happy to have something to do, Lorenz hurried to the ticket counter. When he returned, he and Agnes stood close to one another. They each had much to share but could not speak. Finally, they both said good-bye at the same time. Tears streaked her face as Agnes followed her mother and sister. She waved her handkerchief while the train pulled out of the station, leaving her friends and childhood behind.

In Belgrade Agnes and her family waited for the train to Zagreb. They traveled eight hours to Belgrade and another eight hours to Zagreb. They slept restlessly. When they pulled into the Zagreb station, however, it was much too soon for any of them.

"Are you sure you have enough money?" Drana asked.

"Yes, Mother."

"Write every day," Aga said.

"I will if I can," Agnes said. Drana and Aga hugged Agnes tightly. Then they quickly left the train. Agnes looked out the window at the two women she loved most in the world. They seemed small and forlorn waving their good-byes.

The nuns had arranged for Agnes to travel from Zagreb to the Loreto House in Paris with Betike Kanjc, another young postulant. There Mother Eugene MacAvin, the sister in charge, would interview them. If she recommended them to the mother general, they would go to the motherhouse in Ireland for training and then on to India.

The two young women stared out the window as the train rolled across Austria finally bringing them to Paris, their first step to becoming missionaries in India. In Paris they saw businessmen at their trade, shopkeepers selling their wares, people sightseeing and enjoying the city, priests crossing the streets, women in tight-fitting clothes and heavy makeup standing on street corners, mourners on their way to a funeral, lovers walking hand-in-hand stopping to kiss under a tree. They saw mothers trying to control their children and schoolchildren in their uniforms.

"Just where do I fit in?" Agnes wondered. "God, are you calling me to live behind walls and dedicate all my thoughts to you? Let me be certain, and I will be faithful in thought, word and deed." Agnes had only one goal, to lose herself and find her Lord, to become empty of anything that was not directly from God. She wanted her mind, heart and soul to know the thirst for God that leads to perfect love.

When they knocked on the door of the large old building in Paris where the Loreto sisters lived, Agnes and Betike were both frightened. Agnes prayed that she would not do anything to destroy God's plan for her. "God, I have longed to adore you completely as a nun. If this is your will, please help me."

They were ushered into a large, simply furnished room and told to sit on a plain but comfortable sofa. Agnes was already getting homesick. Maybe God was calling her to do something in Skopje, closer to home. "How weak I am to doubt my calling at the first obstacle. I offer the homesickness to you, my God."

Mother Eugene entered the room with an interpreter from the Yugoslavian embassy. She asked Agnes, "Are you certain God is calling you to be a nun?"

"Yes, Mother, I feel certain."

"And how do you know?"

"Because of the joy. Ever since I became sure of the call I have felt this joy." But as she spoke, all of her joy escaped, and she felt only the sorrow at leaving her beloved family. She was unable to prevent a deep sob. Mother Eugene put her arms around her.

"My dear, it is difficult leaving your home, your family. I remember how I felt when I left mine."

"But I know God wants me to be a missionary, and I never say no to him."

Mother Eugene recommended the girls to the Loreto Abbey at Rathfarnham. Traveling by horse and cart, Agnes was struck by the similarities with Skopje, the many farms, the herds of sheep, the rolling hills. Betike must have thought the same. She said, "It looks so much like home."

The weather was brisk as the countryside readied itself for the onslaught of winter, and Agnes clutched her coat collar to her throat. Her eyes narrowed involuntarily against the swirling dust from the bumpy roads. At last they arrived at the convent, and the elderly driver snapped Agnes out of her reverie. "Here we are my little lasses, all safe and sound." He swung down from the cart and reached for their valises in the rear baggage section. Agnes noticed the kind face of the nun standing at the front gate.

"Agnes Gonxha Bojaxhiu and Betike Kanjc?" she asked. "You must be tired after the long journey. Come, have some food." She helped the girls carry their valises. Agnes and Betike did not understand the woman's words, but they appreciated her kindness. She directed them to their modest quarters and then to the dining room. Absolutely famished, they enjoyed the cooked cabbage with potatoes and homemade bread.

After supper a young nun took them to a pleasant business office, a spacious room with bookshelves lining two entire walls. Behind a modest desk, an elderly sister smiled at them over her glasses. Neither girl knew enough English to understand her warm welcoming speech.

In the ensuing days Agnes and Betike immersed themselves in English classes. Both were hard workers who loved details, and they learned rapidly. One evening Betike entered Agnes's little cell and asked, "How's your English coming along?"

Agnes recited an English limerick almost flawlessly. Her friend giggled. Each day the girls studied English and did their share of cleaning, washing dishes and the various duties they were assigned. After six weeks in Ireland, on November 28, 1928, Agnes and Betike boarded the *Marcha* for India. Ireland would always tug at their hearts. Neither girl was close to any novitiate or nun since no one spoke Serbo-Croatian or Albanian. But both had felt at home in the convent and would always feel a bond with the other women there.

The ship left at four in the afternoon. The sea was calm and the air fresh. The Irish hills rose up in the background. Agnes and Betike shared a cabin that was even smaller than their convent cells. They soon met three young Franciscan sisters who were also going to India. "Let's plan our lives the way it is in the convent," a Franciscan sister suggested. They decided to wake up at 5:00 AM, meet for prayer at 5:50 and go to breakfast together at 7:00.

The trip lasted seven weeks. The ship went through the Suez Canal, the Red Sea, the Indian Ocean and finally the Bay of Bengal. At night the moon shone on the sparkling waves. But days were long and tiresome, and when storms rocked the ship, Agnes and her friends fought off seasickness.

The women were disappointed that there was no Catholic priest on board. They could not receive Holy Communion even on Christmas. But they were determined to celebrate. They improvised a cardboard manger. Every day they sang Christmas carols. On Christmas Eve they recited the rosary before the crib at midnight and ended their evening singing "Adeste Fideles." Stars brightened the sky and the ocean glowed in the moonlight. Agnes felt homesick on her first Christmas away from home, but the fellowship with Betike and the three Franciscan nuns was consoling, and her dream of being Jesus' missionary was coming true. They rejoiced when the ship stopped at Port Said where they attended Mass and received Holy Communion for the first time since they left Ireland.

The ship reached Columbo, Ceylon (now Sri Lanka), on December 27, 1928. Mr. Scalon, the brother of a Loreto sister, was waiting for them at the dock. He took them to a chapel at St. Joseph College. Then he invited them to his home. They recognized Europeans in their elegant clothes while most natives were half-naked and barefoot. Agnes felt sorry for the poor men who pulled their rickshaws through the crowded streets.

The next day they toured Columbo. When they returned to the ship, a Jesuit priest was on board, and now they would have daily Mass. Agnes and her friends celebrated New Year's Eve even though they were homesick.

On New Year's Day they arrived at Madras. Agnes got her first glimpse of India's poor from the ship. The next day the five women visited the city where homeless families slept on mats, old rags or on bare ground. Many people were naked. Some men were bare-chested with a simple loincloth. Often the poor wore fine bracelets on their arms with earrings and a nose ring. They had special marks on their foreheads.

On January 6, 1929, the Feast of the Epiphany, the ship arrived in Calcutta, a region in the northeast corner of India. The Loreto sisters welcoming them on the docks helped Agnes and Betike feel at home. They went directly to the convent chapel to thank God for a safe journey.

After a week in Calcutta Agnes and Betike went to Darjeeling, a beautiful city in the foothills of the Himalayas.

On May 23, 1929, Agnes and Betike officially entered the Order of Loreto. The archbishop of Calcutta reminded them that their new life must be dedicated completely to God.

The mother superior asked, "What name will you take for your new life?"

Agnes said, "I shall be Mary Teresa. Mary for Our Blessed Mother and Teresa for Saint Thérèse of Lisieux of the Child Jesus and the Holy Face, the patron saint of missionaries, and I will be a missionary." She was intrigued by the saint's "little way of spiritual childhood," a path to God through unconditional trust and self-surrender. Agnes's friend, Betike, took Sister Mary Magdalene as her new name. Before she went to bed, Agnes prayed, "Dear Jesus, let me love you with an all-consuming love. Let me bring as many little souls as possible home to you."

3

THE SECOND CALLING

As usual, Sister Teresa performed her tasks single-mindedly. Although she was delighted by a letter from home, she had little time for writing.

On May 25, 1931, Sister Teresa and Sister Mary Magdalene made their first temporary vows. They took the vow of chastity to love Jesus with all their hearts, the vow of poverty to be attached only to the Lord, the vow of obedience to imitate Jesus who always followed his Father's will. The novitiate is a time of preparation for religious life. For Sister Teresa and Sister Mary Magdalene the transition was shocking. After leaving their peaceful mountain homeland, they now faced inconceivable suffering.

Sister Teresa helped the nurses in a small Bengalese hospital. When she entered the crowded waiting room, everyone looked at her hopefully. Many people had open sores. Some were in the last stages of tuberculosis. Mothers held up their babies. She prayed over them.

Although Sister Teresa was happy at the hospital, her superiors sent her to college in Calcutta to obtain her teaching certificate. She observed the terrible poverty, overcrowded streets and chaotic slums called *bustees*.

The Loreto Convent was an oasis of tranquility in the center of a crowded bustee. A concrete wall surrounded the convent and a high school. Inside, students in clean uniforms learned their lessons, laughed and played in their safe world. Some students were orphans or children of broken marriages from all races and communities. But the majority came from wealthy families. The well-cared-for grounds had green grass and swaying palm trees. Looking out her window, Sister Teresa prayed for the poor people.

Sister Teresa had dreamed of teaching school. On her first day the children watched her every move. She rolled up her sleeves, moved everything out of the room, got water and a mop and cleaned the floor.

The children were astonished. Never had they seen a teacher do such a thing. This was India where only lower caste did the cleaning. But Sister Teresa intrigued them and soon the girls were mopping and the boys were carrying clean water.

Sister Teresa's affinity for her students, her sense of humor and ready smile won their love. She was popular with the other teachers.

After nine years in India, on May 24, 1937, Sister Teresa and Sister Mary Magdalene made their final vows at Darjeeling. "Jesus, my love," Sister Teresa sighed, "I am now wed to you. Please fill my heart with so much love that no woman in the world will love her husband as much as I love you."

When Sister Teresa returned to Calcutta, she taught at St. Mary's High School and became director of curriculum.

On September 1, 1939, Nazi Germany invaded Poland. Britain declared war on Germany and, without consulting any Indians, brought India into the war. The Indian Congress, led by Mohandas Gandhi's nonviolent resistance, demanded their freedom. Winston Churchill, prime minister of England, refused.

On December 7, 1941, the Japanese bombed Pearl Harbor and the United States entered the war. President Roosevelt asked Churchill to grant India her independence, but the prime minister again refused. Boats that once brought rice from paddy lands to the cities were forced into military service, cutting off the meager food supply and causing a famine that took over four million lives.

During the Second World War Sister Teresa was St. Mary's principal and directed the Daughters of St. Anne, the Indian religious order attached to the Loreto sisters. She became friends with Father Henry, pastor of St. Teresa's Church, and they worked together with the young people in the Sodality of Our Lady to help the poor.

Before the partition of India into separate Hindu and Muslim nations, Calcutta suffered immensely because its population was almost equally divided between the two religions. There were often riots.

England was waiting for India to form its own government. Gandhi and the Indian Congress wanted a united India where people of all religions lived in peace. Muslim leaders wanted a separate Muslim state so that Muslims who were the minority would be safe.

The newly formed Muslim League declared August 16, 1946, "Direct Action Day," aggravating the hostility between the two groups.

Ma Charu, a cook at St. Mary's High School, told Sister Teresa, "The food hasn't arrived, and we have three hundred hungry mouths to feed."

"Pray," Teresa said, "Pray hard."

Sister Teresa went into the streets to buy food. This was the first time she had left the convent alone. She discovered a city frozen by violence. Middle-class people were afraid to step outside their doors. Businesses were closed down. Shops were set afire with their owners inside. Men and women had been stabbed and left to bleed to death. Bodies were tossed into sewers. A truckload of soldiers stopped her. "Why are you in the street, lady? Don't you see how dangerous it is?"

"I have three hundred students with nothing to eat."

"We have rice, lady. Get in the truck, and we'll take you back to your school." The soldiers unloaded the bags of rice for her.

"Ma Charu, your prayers worked," she told the cook who hurried into the kitchen to prepare the rice. At least five thousand people died that day, and over fifteen thousand were wounded.

On September 10, 1946, Sister Teresa and the other nuns were on a train to Darjeeling for their annual retreat. As the train puffed its way up the mountainside, Teresa closed her eyes, and images of the horrors of Calcutta passed through her mind. She saw abandoned children lying on the sidewalks. She watched living skeletons searching through garbage bins for food. She saw a mother, driven insane by hunger and despair, trying to strangle her own son. Suddenly, she heard Jesus' voice inside her. He was on the cross. "I thirst," he said. "Teresa, I thirst for your love."

"My Lord, I love you," she said.

"Quench my thirst in the poorest of the poor. Follow me into the streets. Be my hands and tend my sick. Be my feet and visit my lonely, my sick, my prisoners. Be my voice and calm the distressed, comfort the afflicted, help the dying to come home to me."

Was she losing her mind? Jesus had called her to leave the world, to be a nun in a convent and to follow him on an inward journey. How could he ask her to return to the world? Her superiors would never allow it, and she had taken a vow of obedience. "Am I, a nun, threatened by tuberculosis, to leave the convent where I feel so close to you, and go out alone?" she asked.

And he repeated the call, "Teresa, do you love me?"

"Oh, yes, Lord."

"Then feed my sheep. Come follow me."

"Yes, Lord," she whispered. First she said it in her head, then in her heart.

"Yes, my Lord. Whatever you ask for I will give you willingly, and whatever you give me I will take willingly. I am all yours. Cut me into little pieces, and every little piece will be yours."

"I love you, Teresa." Jesus' voice was clear and full of compassion. The eyes of her soul saw the way he looked at her with infinite love. Teresa was faced with Jesus' all-consuming, unconditional love for her. It was as if there was no one else in the world but Jesus and herself. "Whatever you do to the least of my people, you do to me," Jesus repeated over and over in her head.

"Your love is all I will ever need." She knew the fire that Jesus had lit in her soul would burn forever. From it she would draw the strength to do his will for as long as she lived. During the retreat Teresa stayed to herself praying and meditating. She never doubted that God was calling her once more. She had never said no to Jesus, and she was not going to begin now.

"Are you ill, Sister Teresa?" asked Sister Mary Magdalene. "You are so quiet, and you aren't smiling."

"I'm sorry, Sister Magdalene," she said. "I'm trying to determine if God wants me to leave the convent."

Sister Mary Magdalene cut her off. "God called you to the convent. He would never call you away."

"I believe that is what he is doing," Sister Teresa said. "I know where I belong but I don't know how to get there." Her mother wrote, "Do not forget that you went there to help the poor. Do you remember old Filja? She is covered with sores, but what bothers her most is being alone in the world."

Sister Teresa could not begin her new mission until she had permission and was released from her convent. She wrote plans for her future work. She described the call and how she was to care for the poor in a spirit of trust, surrender and joy. She would not work behind walls, and those who joined would be bound to satiate Jesus' thirst for souls by wholehearted free service to the poor.

She took the notes to her spiritual director, Father Celest Van Exem, a Jesuit priest. He said, "I suggest you ask the archbishop."

Archbishop Ferdinand Perier of Calcutta received Teresa like a true father, with kindness and understanding. He listened to her attentively. Then, he said, "I'm sorry. I must say no, absolutely no." She told her superior of the archbishop's refusal and returned to her work, but day and night she prayed for guidance.

The year 1947 was a year of waiting for Sister Teresa. It was a year of bloodshed for India. On August 15, 1947, England granted India independence, but Mohandas Gandhi, whose peaceful resistance had led India to freedom, did not celebrate. India broke out in riots as it was divided into two nations, Pakistan for the Muslims, and what was left of India for the Hindus. The border between India and the newly formed East Pakistan cut through Bengal, and millions of Hindus and Muslims found themselves in enemy territory. There was a mass exodus as they attempted to reach safety, and as a result, millions of Hindu refugees fleeing East Pakistan poured into over-crowded Calcutta. They brought with them only their desperate problems.

God continued to call Sister Teresa to care for the poor. When she returned to Archbishop Perier, he asked, "Do you know what you're asking? Are you strong enough for this work? A European woman alone in the slums would not be accepted."

"I am convinced that it is God's work and not mine. I am completely at his disposal. Without him I can do nothing. With him all things are possible."

This time the archbishop advised her to seek the permission of the Loreto motherhouse. Mother Gertrude recognized God's voice in Sister Teresa's letter and said, "If God is calling you, I give you my permission. I want you to know that we love you, and there will always be a place for you with us."

Sister Teresa's request was forwarded to Rome. A nun living and working outside the convent system was unheard of, but she waited, teaching her regular classes and working with the poor.

During the ensuing months, Sister Teresa did not forget her quest, but she had every reason to believe the Vatican had.

In September of 1947 Pakistan invaded Kashmir, starting a war between India and Pakistan. This war caused great economic losses to India and fed the religious-nationalistic bitterness with terrible consequences. Many of the poorest were uprooted and forced to travel long distances with little food and water, carrying their sick, their elderly, their babies. Tempers were short and the country was primed for violence. Whole villages were burned, wives and daughters were raped, some committed suicide.

In the midst of all this suffering, Sister Teresa felt even more frustrated. Although the call to help the poor was always in her mind, she could do nothing until the pope released her from her commitment to the Loreto sisters.

Even when she was a young girl, Teresa had lung problems, and now she had tuberculosis. Her superiors sent her to Asansol, about three hours from Calcutta by train. She taught geography there and worked in the garden.

Trouble broke out at St. Mary's between the students and teachers. When the authorities could not settle the dispute, Archbishop Perier sent for Sister Teresa. She met with the student leaders and within half an hour the problems were solved.

But Sister Teresa's chosen country faced other problems. On January 30, 1948, at 5:00 PM, Mohandas Gandhi was on his way to evening prayer. A Hindu fanatic walked up to him, bowed low, then fired three shots at close range. Gandhi said, "Oh, God," and died.

That same year on August 8 Father Van Exem asked Sister Teresa, "Could you meet me in the convent parlor after Mass? When she entered, he said, "Sister Teresa, I have your reply from Rome."

She turned pale. "May I go to the chapel before we read it?"

When she returned, he handed her the letter from Pope Pius

XII. Her hands trembled as she read it. It gave her permission to "live alone outside the cloister among the poor of Calcutta with God alone as her protector and guide."

"Can I go to the slums now?" Sister Teresa asked Father Van Exem.

"It is not so simple," he explained. "You are now under obedience to the archbishop of Calcutta."

He saw her disappointment. "Don't worry," he said. "Your biggest obstacle has been overcome. All you need is a little more patience."

That evening Sister Teresa came to Father Van Exem in the convent chapel. "Father, I'd like you to bless these for me, please." She held up an inexpensive white sari, the type poor Bengali women wore, a small cross and a rosary.

Sister Cenacle, mother superior of the convent where Sister Teresa had lived the last seventeen years, stood next to her, crying. Father Van Exem told her, "Don't worry, sister, if this is not God's will, Sister Teresa will return to us."

Archbishop Perier asked Sister Teresa, "Where will you begin?"

"Father Van Exem has suggested I speak to you about going to Patna to work with the Medical Mission Sisters so I can learn basic nursing skills."

"That is an excellent idea, Sister Teresa."

That night she wrote the Medical Mission Sisters. On August 15, 1948, she received an invitation to visit them. Leaving the Sisters of Loreto was the hardest thing she had ever done. It was even more difficult than leaving her family and her country when she was eighteen years old. She had felt so close to Jesus in this lovely convent, and the sisters had become her family. Everyone at the convent of Loreto loved Sister Teresa and was sad to see her go.

Her students wept. "Why does it have to be Sister Teresa?" they asked.

When the time came for her to go, the girls sang farewell songs in Bengali. Sister Teresa cried with them. Then she went to the chapel. She removed her European habit with its full skirt reaching to the floor, the white coif around the head and the long black veil. She slipped into her white sari that Father Van Exem had blessed and a plain pair of sandals.

As she left the convent grounds, she felt lonelier than she ever had felt in her life, but she knew she was doing God's will. No one saw her slip out the gate in her sari. She left the warmth of the convent, the spiritual life, the friendship and loving concern and put her complete trust in Jesus.

Once again Sister Teresa was at a train station starting a long journey, but this time there was no one to say good-bye. She traveled 240 miles north to study practical nursing. When she left the train in Patna, an ancient city on the Ganges River, three Medical Mission Sisters welcomed her.

The Holy Family Hospital was staffed by the Medical Mission Sisters who were doctors, nurses, laboratory technicians and dietitians. Traditionally, the Catholic church did not allow nuns to do surgery or to deliver babies in its hospitals. Mother Dengel, an Austrian-born woman and head of the Medical Mission Sisters, had obtained permission from the pope for her sister-doctors to practice surgery and midwifery, so she understood Sister Teresa's desire to be a nun in a new way.

"I hope to start a congregation that will live with the poor in India," Sister Teresa told Mother Dengel. "We will wear simple inexpensive saris and sandals, sleep on mattresses on the floor and eat only rice and salt."

"Oh, no, Sister!" Mother Dengel said. "You will be committing a serious sin if you have your sisters work until they are exhausted, exposing themselves to the illnesses of the poor without eating the proper food and getting the necessary rest. The poor work very little because they have no strength and are often sick. Don't you want your sisters to be strong and able to labor well?"

Sister Teresa realized Mother Dengel was right.

The hospital was a converted school building, two stories high. The operating and delivery room was in a smaller building nearby. The Medical sisters were too busy to spend much time talking with Sister Teresa. They assigned her a cell and a chair in the dining and community room. She was on her own.

Whenever they had an emergency, a new admission, an operation or delivery, they called Sister Teresa when they called the doctor. She held the patient's hand during painful or frightening procedures, consoled crying children and helped any way she could.

Her Bengali was fluent, and she was learning Hindi. The Medical sisters were invited to weddings, celebrations, wakes or thanksgivings for recoveries. Sister Teresa enjoyed going along.

Every evening Sister Teresa joined the Medical sisters for recreation. Prayer time for the Medical sisters ended at 9:00 PM. Their meals were simple but sufficient, and they ate plenty of protein. They took a daily nap. Everyone had one day of rest and those who worked on Sunday took another day off. They wore white cotton habits and veils, which they changed at least once a day due to the heat.

While Sister Teresa was at Holy Family Hospital, she received a visitor who was to be important in her work. Jacqueline de Decker, a European woman dressed in a simple sari much like Sister Teresa, found her in the chapel deep in prayer. The woman quietly slipped into a pew and knelt.

Both women were born in Europe and were devoted to India's poor. They had both adopted the Indian habits of dressing, eating while sitting on the floor and sleeping on simple mattresses. Both women served anyone in need regardless of caste, religion, sex or age.

When Sister Teresa noticed Jacqueline, she ushered her outside the chapel so they could talk.

"I was born in Belgium," Jacqueline said. "I am a nurse and I cared for wounded British troops during the war. For a while I worked with Gandhi. Recently, I have been living alone, and the Indians have accepted me. But I want God to use me to help India in some way."

Sister Teresa's complete trust in God and her insistence that it was his work renewed Jacqueline's strength. The two women worked together in the Patna hospital and became close friends.

The week before Christmas in 1948 Sister Teresa returned to Calcutta. The Medical sisters gave her a strong pair of sandals as a going-away gift.

"I wish I could go with you," Jacqueline, who was suffering from a medical ailment, said. "But my doctors say I must return to Belgium for treatment. When my health is better I'll join you."

Back in Belgium Jacqueline wrote, "It will take longer than I expected, but with God's help I shall eventually join you."

Father Van Exem obtained temporary shelter for Sister Teresa with the Little Sisters of the Poor. She helped the Little Sisters care for the elderly. Then she ventured out into the bustees, carrying her lunch since she had no money for food.

That day Sister Teresa started an open-air school in Motijhil, a slum in Calcutta. The first day she had five pupils, all teenagers, but none had ever been to school. She wrote the Bengali alphabet on the ground with a stick. At noon she gave the students milk. Most of them had never seen soap before and were overjoyed when she gave each of them a bar. She got water and showed them how to use the soap.

The next day some girls from St. Mary's came to help her. When she started the work, Sister Teresa had only five rupees (about seventy cents), but people brought her money and supplies.

She taught the alphabet to children who would probably never own a book, and taught children how to use soap even though they would never be able to afford it.

Little by little, God showed her what to do.

One day walking home from the bustees, Sister Teresa met a priest who asked for a contribution. She gave him her last rupee. That evening the same priest brought her an envelope with fifty rupees. She knew that God had blessed the work.

4

Missionaries of Charity

A parishioner called Father Henry. "This is Michael Gomes. My mother is dying." After giving Mrs. Gomes the last rites, Father Henry told him of Sister Teresa and her need for a small room to begin her work.

Michael's eight-year-old daughter, Mabel, said, "The whole upstairs is empty. She could live here."

Michael gave Father Henry a tour of the mansion. Then he asked, "Could she use this space?"

"She wants to live the way the poorest people live."

"But a nun should live in a nice place," Michael said.

Sister Teresa thought the house was too nice and too big. However, after a long desperate search, she accepted an upstairs room.

Early in 1949 Sister Teresa arrived with Ma Charu, the old cook from St. Mary's. Michael Gomes refused to accept money.

Father Henry gave her a corner at a nearby church for an outdoor dispensary. She asked Michael Gomes where she could get medicine. "We have a dispensary. Now we need something to dispense."

"I know someone who might help," Michael said. "I haven't met him but we have spoken on the phone." Michael and Sister

Teresa went out with her list of medicines. Because their order was so large, the manager waited on them himself. When he told her the price, Sister Teresa said, "Since these are for the poor, I would like to have them for free."

"You came to the wrong place, lady," he said. "Let me finish my work."

Sister Teresa prayed her rosary. Michael Gomes sat next to her. When she finished praying, she stood up to go. The manager brought her three parcels. "Here is all your medicine. It is a gift from the company."

"God will bless you," Sister Teresa said.

In the streets beggars followed Sister Teresa. Starving orphans called, "No father! No mother! Give money! Give food!" People with one eye, one leg, lepers, living skeletons pointed to their mouths to show they were hungry. Some were naked. Many could not walk. Some crawled on their hands and knees. She approached those lying on the pavement. She could not tell if they were alive or dead.

Before she had sisters to help her, Sister Teresa would take Michael Gomes's young daughter or his niece with her. They left early in the morning and returned for lunch. One day after a big storm they returned late and Mrs. Gomes was worried. Sister Teresa was drenched. She said, "I'm sorry the girls got wet."

She told of a woman standing in water above her knees, holding a bowl over her dying child. "Because she could not pay eight rupees rent for that miserable room, the landlord tore down the roof and left the poor woman and her sick child in the pouring rain."

The next day Sister Teresa searched for a home for the dying. She walked until her legs and feet ached. She wrote in her diary, "How exhausted the poor must get, walking around in search of food or medicine. I have been tempted by the thought of the comfortable life of the Loreto convent."

"My God, because of my free choice and for love of you alone, I will do whatever you demand."

Sister Teresa prayed for helpers. Unable to find a place for her abandoned dying, she brought them to the Gomes's house. She washed filthy babies whose families had no water and could not afford soap.

One morning a beautiful young Bengali girl in an elegant sari knocked at the door. Her name was Subhasini Das, a former student of Sister Teresa's. She had a flawless complexion, luxurious black hair, a radiant smile and sparkling brown eyes. She said, "Sister Teresa, I want to live with you and help with the work." Sister Teresa took Subhasini's smooth, soft hands in hers.

"Look at my hands," she said. "See how red and rough they are. And you would have to give up your beautiful saris." She led Subhasini upstairs and showed her the poor who shared the room. "This life demands great sacrifice."

"I have thought of nothing else." the girl said. "Please accept me." Sister Teresa saw the qualities she wanted in her future missionaries: healthy mind and body, ability to learn, common sense, natural joy and unfailing good humor.

"Come back on St. Joseph's day," she said, testing her vocation. On March 19, 1949, Subhasini returned in a simple sari with no makeup or jewelry. Sister Teresa handed her a cheap cotton sari like her own. "What name have you chosen?"

"If you don't mind, I want to be Sister Agnes." Sister Teresa was touched. This was the beginning of her new order. She was now Mother Teresa.

One month later along came Magdalena Gomes (not related to Michael Gomes), another former student from St. Mary's. She took the name Sister Gertrude. She was studying medicine and having trouble with the required mathematics. Mother Teresa gave her a crash course, and she passed the examination to become a doctor.

Then came Sister Dorothy, another graduate of St. Mary's. She was followed by yet another former student, Sister Margaret Mary, from East Pakistan who did not know English. Mother had her speaking the language in a few months.

Also among the first to join Mother Teresa was Agnes Vincent, a woman from a well-to-do Bengali family. When she was in the tenth grade, Mother Teresa had taken her to the Motijihl bustee. As they walked through the overcrowded, filthy slum, Mother told her someone should care for these poor, neglected people. And by God's graces, she became Sister Florence and came to help Mother Teresa care for them.

Another young woman, Beatrice Rosario, joined Mother although her family strongly opposed the idea. They could not understand her desire to work in the bustees. But she became Sister Bernard. Together the sisters went from door to door gathering food to feed the hungry.

Michael Gomes watched his upper floor become a real convent. He was religious and loved having so much prayer in his home. The sisters wore the plain white cotton sari with a blue border and a crucifix held on with a safety pin. They all cut their hair. Mother Teresa and her first twelve girls got up at 5:30 every morning, attended Mass and by 7:30 were in the bustees.

Doctors and nurses volunteered. The community grew. Although most novices were middle-class Indian girls, some from the rich upper class and some Anglo-Indians joined. When a sister with chicken pox had to be separated from the others, Mother asked Michael Gomes for another room. "They are all at your disposal," he replied. Slowly, Mother's sisters took over the entire upper floor. Now there were thirty sisters and only two bathrooms. St. Teresa's, a nearby parish, sent builders who put up bathing cubicles on the roof.

The Gomes family heard the sisters' laughter all over the house.

The girls ran and played hopscotch and tug-of-war. But when the bell rang, they stopped whatever they were doing to pray. A bell rang when it was time to eat. And again when it was time to go out. There was no regular work schedule. As they saw a need, they did all they could to alleviate it.

Mother tutored the sisters who were still in school. She insisted that they go to bed early, but she herself wrote letters, made plans and worked on her constitution late every night.

"I've chosen the name Missionaries of Charity because we are carriers of God's love. Our only possessions will be two cotton saris, underwear, sandals, a crucifix, a metal bucket for washing and a straw mat for our bed. Then we will be ready to go anywhere we are needed."

"We will not attempt to convert people of other faiths to Christianity or other Christians to Catholicism," Mother said. "We will see every human being as Christ and we will help Hindus to be better Hindus, Muslims to be better Muslims and Christians to be better Christians."

The sisters lived the Mass by touching Jesus in the broken bodies of the poor and feeding him in the starving people. "This is all Jesus told us," Mother said. "Love one another as I have loved you."

Father Henry Julien, one of Mother Teresa's advisers, and some boys from his parish built an altar and candlesticks for the sisters' chapel. Father Van Exem gave Mother a picture of the Immaculate Heart of Mary, which she hung above the altar. Also above the altar were the words "I Thirst." Mother Teresa told her sisters, "'I thirst' is Jesus saying 'I love you.' Until you know how Jesus thirsts for you, you can't know who he wants to be for you, or who he wants you to be."

The sisters called their home the "Upper Room" since it was on the second floor and it resembled the upper room where Christ and his apostles ate the Last Supper.

The sisters felt their oneness in the Lord. They prayed, studied, slept, ate, talked, sang, played, cooked, washed clothes, scrubbed floors, repaired clothes and made bandages together. English was their common language.

Father Henry and Father Van Exem helped Mother Teresa prepare her constitution for the Holy Father in Rome. On October 7, 1950, the Feast of the Rosary, Father Van Exem read the letter from Rome declaring the Missionaries of Charity an official church organization.

They continued going to the bustees every morning. They took the cramped, suffocating trams or buses. They prayed their rosaries as they traveled. When Mother asked, "How far did you go?" the sisters answered, "Two rosaries," or "Three rosaries," depending on the distance.

One evening Michael Gomes said, "Mother, you remember my niece, Agnes, who went with you to the bustees when you first came here?"

"Of course I remember little Agnes. She always said she wanted to give her life to the poor."

"Well, Agnes is in Holy Family hospital in Patna. She has tuberculosis, and she may be dying." He continued, "Agnes wants only one thing: to be a Missionary of Charity."

"But she is so ill," Mother said.

"Isn't there any way she could take vows?"

"Let's speak with the archbishop," Mother suggested. After praying together, they visited him, and he gave permission for Agnes to enter the order.

On October 3, 1952, right before Agnes's twentieth birthday, Mother Teresa and Agnes's father joined the young girl in her hospital room. Agnes was very thin and pale. In spite of her pain, she was cheerful.

She took the vows of poverty, obedience, chastity and the

fourth vow of free service to the poorest of the poor. She chose to be Sister Maria Goretti for a recently canonized Italian teenager stabbed to death defending her virginity.

"Sister Maria Goretti, you are now a Missionary of Charity, and your prayers and sufferings will enable us active missionaries to do beautiful things for Jesus."

"I have never been so happy," Sister Maria Goretti said.

"It is your wedding day," Mother said.

Since their first meeting in 1948 in Patna, Mother Teresa and Jacqueline de Decker had corresponded. Jacqueline would have been Mother's first nun if she had not had serious health problems.

When Jacqueline realized that she could never return to India, she became depressed. But gradually she accepted God's will.

In the autumn of 1952, Mother Teresa wrote Jacqueline: "Why not become spiritually bound to our society? While we work in the slums, you share in the merit, the prayers and the work. I need souls like yours to pray and suffer for the work."

Jacqueline realized that God was giving her a special role in his work. She was eager to be spiritually united with the Missionaries of Charity.

That Christmas Sister Maria Goretti wanted her uncle, Michael Gomes, to visit her. When he arrived in Patna, the Medical Missionaries told him, "The doctors can't understand how your niece is staying alive. Both of her lungs have been eaten away." But when she recognized him, a smile lit up her face.

"Hello, Sister Maria Goretti," he said.

"I'm a Missionary of Charity," she said proudly. "Now my suffering goes to save souls, Uncle Michael. As sick as I am, I can do something that matters. Nothing is more important than saving souls."

5

Nirmal Hriday

In 1952 Mother Teresa searched the teeming streets of Calcutta for the needy. She appeared older than her forty-two years with her back bent and her face weathered, but she had the energy of an athlete. Although she said her rosary as she walked, she never missed someone in trouble. Mother Teresa found a woman lying in rubbish, half-eaten by rats. "My own son put me here!" she cried. Mother carried her to the nearest hospital.

Just as citizens of other nations watch violent news reports without emotion, the wealthier Indians ignored the poor dying in the streets.

At the hospital a receptionist said, "We can't admit this woman. We take only curable patients. She is dying."

Mother said, "I won't move until you admit her."

A few weeks earlier a naked beggar about thirteen years old lay dying by the roadside when someone took the boy to the hospital. Since he was homeless, naked and near death, the hospital sent him back to the gutter where he died alone. The Calcutta newspapers picked up the story, and people who had stepped over dying bodies wept when they read it.

To avoid unfavorable publicity, the hospital admitted the woman Mother Teresa brought them. The receptionist said, "We'll take her in, but you are robbing someone we might have saved." Mother Teresa prayed her rosary. Soon the receptionist said, "The woman died."

Mother left.

She went to the health department and said, "Give me a place where people can die with dignity."

A city official said, "Newspaper articles show people dying in the streets. Something must be done." Many of the officials had heard of Mother's order. They huddled together while Mother said her rosary.

Then they said, "Mother, you have a choice between two buildings. One is near your convent. The other was a pilgrims' rest home next door to the temple of Kali, the Hindu goddess of death."

"I'd like to see the rest home," Mother said.

"Wouldn't the other building be more convenient, Mother?"

"The rest home is sacred to Indians," Mother said. "They feel close to God there, and that's more important than our convenience. It's Jesus we care for in the homeless, and he never worried about whether dying for us on the cross was convenient."

The health officials showed Mother Teresa the ancient pilgrims' hostel. She looked at the dusty old building, empty except for some rowdy men. It was hundreds of years old. There were two great rooms at right angles to each other, joined by a passage. A strong musty odor permeated the air. The windows were small and placed high on the thick walls, not permitting much sunlight. Mother imagined the two rooms filled with dying people lovingly cared for by her sisters.

"This will be the best place for Indian people to rest before they go to heaven. Yes, this is the building I want."

"But Mother," a health official said, "you haven't seen the other building."

"There is no need."

"When will you open?" the man asked.

"Tomorrow."

Mother Teresa knelt on the hard, dirty floor to thank God and Our Lady. Then she hurried home to share the good news. The sisters prayed, had a small meal, collected cleaning utensils and rushed to the hostel. They scrubbed floors, washed walls and put down mats. Working late into the night, they were exhausted but joyful when they finished.

"We'll name our home Nirmal Hriday, the place of the Immaculate Heart of Mary, since Jesus' mother found it for us," Mother said.

The next morning they welcomed their first patient, a woman found lying outside the hospital where Mother had taken the woman she had found earlier. The house was soon filled with dying people.

At first the Brahmin (upper-class) priests spied on Mother and her sisters. Rumors spread that Mother wanted to convert Hindu people to Christianity. In truth she allowed people to die with their own religious rituals—Muslim, Hindu, Buddhist, Catholic, Protestant, Jewish or any other.

Some young Hindu men decided to get Mother Teresa and her sisters out of the pilgrims' rest home. They threw stones. A stone just missed a dying woman. Mother went to the Brahmin priests. "Kill me if you wish, but please don't harm the dying."

The young men went to the local congress committee, saying, "We must stop this foreign woman from forcing our poor to become Christians."

"I'll get her out of Kali's house," the commissioner promised. "But first I want to see the situation."

When he arrived at the home, Mother Teresa was caring for a dying patient. Ignoring the terrible odor in the room, she was putting medicine on an open wound covered with maggots. "What can I do for you?" she asked.

"Nothing, thank you. I just want to look around."

Mother continued caring for the dying man.

The boys again asked the commissioner to remove the sisters. The commissioner said, "I will put this lady out, but you must get your mothers and sisters to do the work she is doing."

He led the boys to Kali's statue. "Here's a statue of your Kali." Then he brought them back to see Mother Teresa, who was still treating the dying man. "Here is the living Kali," he said. "How can we throw her out?" Defeated, the boys left. After that, the police commissioner protected Mother and Nirmal Hriday.

One day Mother found a crowd outside the Kali temple around a Brahmin priest lying in his own mess. No one would touch him because he had cholera, an infectious disease. Mother carried him into the house where she and the sisters cared for him.

One morning Mother Teresa was making her rounds, speaking to each patient in Hindi or Bengali. "How are you today?" "You are looking much better." "Are you eating?" She came to a young man who was close to death. A sister rubbed his forehead. Mother Teresa reached down, straightened his head on the pillow and asked, "Does he have any family?"

"No, Mother."

"Does anyone know he's here?"

"He has no one, Mother." Mother shook her head sadly. She touched him gently, then continued on her rounds. Before she left for the day, Mother returned to the young man. She looked at his face. "So peaceful," she said. "He's all ready to go home."

Being surrounded by so much love, even the Hindu priest with cholera changed his attitude. He thanked the sisters. When the other temple priests visited him, they were astonished at how much he had changed.

One day he said, "Please give me your blessing, Mother." She wet his lips with water from the Ganges River, a sacred ritual for the Hindus. "God bless you, my friend," she said. "You are going home to God." The man smiled. "Thank you, Mother Teresa." Then he died.

One of the sisters touched him gently. "Just think, Mother. He is seeing the face of God." Mother's attention was fixed completely on the face of the Hindu priest. She was seeing Christ in his mother's arms after he was taken down from the cross. She lovingly touched his bare feet, then covered him and said, "It is finished."

6

SHISHU BHAVAN

MOTHER EXPLAINED HER IDEAS FOR THE SICK AND SUFFERING LINKS TO Jacqueline de Decker in January, 1953. "I want especially the paralyzed, the crippled, the incurables to bring souls to Jesus. Each sister will have a second self." Mother Teresa asked Jacqueline to find a sick and suffering partner for the ten novices who would soon be professed.

Jacqueline was in the hospital after her thirtieth operation. She found a suffering second self for each sister. Mother Teresa wrote, "Our Lord loves you very much to give you so great a part in his suffering. Be brave and cheerful and offer much to bring many souls to God."

Although she was in constant pain, Jacqueline traveled to various countries and joined Sick and Suffering Coworkers with Missionaries of Charity. She wrote comforting letters to all who confided in her.

Many women joined the order. They occupied the entire upper floor of the Gomes's house, slept side by side like sardines and prayed for a permanent house. A man offered Mother a small dilapidated house. When she said, "The house is ready to collapse," he jumped up and down to demonstrate the sturdiness and disappeared through the floor.

When Father Henry learned a large home on his street was for sale, he visited the owner, a wealthy Muslim. Three houses shared a courtyard at 54A Lower Circular Road. The street was crowded with pedestrians, streetcars, vendors, children at play, people rushing to work. The owner greeted Father Henry, "I studied with the Jesuits, Father. I have always loved priests."

Father told him about Mother Teresa and asked, "What do you want for the place?"

"To you I will sell it for 7,500 rupees, less than I paid for the land." Although the archbishop was having cataract surgery, Father Henry explained the urgency to him and within three days they had the house.

When Mother Teresa saw the place, she said, "Father, it is much too big." Father Henry smiled. "Mother, one day you will ask where to put all of your people."

Sister Maria Goretti, Michael Gomes's little niece, died on September 8, 1953, and was buried in Patna near Holy Family Hospital. "Now we have a Missionary of Charity in heaven," Mother Teresa said.

In 1954 Mother Teresa met Ann Blaikie, a British woman who helped organize the Coworkers, a lay organization that helped the Missionaries of Charity to create a bond of love encircling the entire world. Ann lived with her husband and two children in Calcutta, and was expecting another baby. She could no longer work full time in the shop where she and her friends sold crafts made by poor people. While her servants cared for the children, she wondered how to help the needy and keep herself busy until the new baby arrived.

Ann's friend Margaret McKenzie, who was also pregnant, went with her to see Mother, who took them to Nirmal Hriday, the home for the dying. Ann and her friend offered to collect toys for Mother's annual Christmas party. Mother immediately accepted their offer.

Then she said, "Could you get dresses, shirts and shoes for all our Christian children at Christmas?"

Ann found other European and American women in Calcutta, and they sold homemade angels to buy the clothes Mother wanted, and they repaired and painted old toys.

After the Christmas party Mother Teresa thanked them and then asked, "Now could you help with the Muslim children's annual festival?" After that there would be the Hindu children's party.

They were needed all year. They called themselves the Marian Society. Indians and Anglo-Indians joined. Many helpers lived in big homes with servants and luxuries. Although they were surrounded by poverty, they didn't see it until they began working with Mother.

Mother Teresa found a dog dragging a newborn baby in its mouth. She brought the baby home. It soon died, but it had known a few moments of love. She found babies in garbage bins, in gutters, on doorsteps and in churches left by mothers who could not feed them. More mothers were having children they could not care for. Midwives brought unwanted babies to Mother. She was looking for a children's home.

In 1955 she opened Shishu Bhavan, her first home for unwanted children who would otherwise die alone in the streets. It was a plain two-story building a few blocks from the motherhouse. A high wall stood in front of the building with an iron gate for cars and a small brown door for pedestrians. In the open courtyard the sisters placed a statue of Our Lady. Children played everywhere. They covered the walls with drawings and scrawled their own names.

Inside the main building a long row of cribs held premature infants. Each new baby was washed, fed, given whatever medicine it needed and dressed. The sisters wrapped them in colorful blankets knitted or quilted by the Marian Society. The babies wore tiny booties small enough for dolls.

"Never refuse any child a home," Mother said. "Remember each child is the Baby Jesus." Even if the babies slept three or more in a crib, the sisters always made room for another.

Sometimes people who died in Nirmal Hriday left children. Mothers put babies on the doorstep of the motherhouse or the children's home. Parents brought children saying, "Mother, please take care of them. We have no food, and they are sick." The police, social workers and doctors sent children. "Just as Our Lady and Saint Joseph made a beautiful home for Jesus in Nazareth, we must provide a loving home for these children."

Many children were dying. Some had tuberculosis and others were starving. Many of the infants were victims of attempted abortions, most too tiny to live. Mother Teresa would hand a baby to a helper. "Let her know a little love before she goes home to her Father."

Many babies died soon after their arrival. "I don't care what people say about how many of our babies die," Mother said. "These babies must not die uncared for and unloved." Usually the sisters spent a week caring for a baby before it smiled. Shishu Bhavan had enough space for one hundred children at a time. Mother Teresa kept teenage girls at Shishu Bhavan, but sent older boys to a boys' town run by the Catholic church.

A little boy whose parents had both died refused to eat and would not talk or play with anyone. He smiled when a certain sister came near him, so Mother let that sister care for him while someone else did her work. The little boy began to eat and to play with other children.

One day Mother Teresa found a little girl about six years old alone in Calcutta. Mother could tell that she hadn't eaten for several days, so she gave her a crust of bread. The little girl ate slowly, one crumb at a time. "Go on, eat the bread," Mother Teresa told the child.

The little girl said, "I'm afraid to eat it all. When the bread is finished, I will be hungry again."

"No," Mother Teresa promised. "We will make sure you have food."

Once Mother took in a family of six children to raise. The father had disappeared. The mother kept the children alive until she starved to death. The children did not know what to do with their mother's body. Finally the neighbors took it, but they were too poor to care for the children. Rita, the oldest girl, who was fourteen, was determined to keep the family together, but the baby just lay without a sound. A newspaper published their story.

Right away Mother Teresa called. The newspaper had collected seven thousand rupees (about seven hundred dollars) for the children. Mother put five thousand rupees in the bank for Rita's dowry and used the rest for the children. The sisters raised them.

Many Indian children could not go to school, having only rags to wear and never enough food. They had no pencils or paper and almost no light by which to study.

Mother was determined that every child in her care who could learn would get an education or training to help them earn a living. A wealthy Hindu lady paid the tuition for Mother Teresa's first ten children.

Shishu Bhavan was full of laughter. The sisters carried the children in their arms, gave them piggyback rides and swung them in the air. Shishu Bhavan became the center for work in Calcutta. Next to the main building a nurses' office stayed busy and a huge kitchen fed seven thousand people every day; if the sisters did not cook, the people had no food. One day a sister said, "Mother, we have no food." Mother prayed. Soon two trucks drove up loaded with bread. The government had shut down the schools for one day and given Mother Teresa's poor the bread the children usually ate.

The sisters invited unwed mothers to stay at Shishu Bhavan until their babies were born. If the mothers could not care for their babies, the sisters would find a good home for them.

One morning a man came for Mother Teresa. "Mother, please help me! My wife is about to kill our baby!" Mother and the man rushed to the hospital. The man said, "We have a hard time feeding all of our children so my wife wants to kill our unborn baby." They got to the hospital in time, but the wife was already on the operating table. Mother Teresa said, "Please don't let your baby die. God takes care of the flowers and the birds. These little children are his life."

The woman began to cry. "I didn't want to hurt my baby, Mother. But I already have four daughters and it is so hard to take care of them."

"The sisters and I will help you," Mother promised. The woman climbed down from the operating table and the three of them left the hospital. Five months later, the woman gave birth to her first son and the whole family rejoiced.

Mother Teresa began teaching couples how to use self-control and natural family planning. "Isn't it strange for nuns to be teaching birth control?" a woman asked.

Mother laughed. "Who is better able to teach a method of self-control than we who have taken vows of chastity?"

Once while Mother had ninety-five cartons of powdered milk in the courtyard, rain poured down for five days. "What are you doing, Lord?" cried Mother Teresa. "The milk is outside!" The worried sisters prayed. When the rain stopped, they rushed out to inspect the damage. The boxes were floating in water, but the milk was dry. When Mother started opening a box with a broken lid, she said, "God, what happened to this one?" But not one drop of water had entered the broken box.

"What earthly spouse would take such good care of his family?" Mother asked.

A child once came to the children's home around midnight. She was in tears just outside the gate. "What's wrong?" Mother asked.

"My mother doesn't want me," the little girl sobbed. "My father doesn't want me. Nobody wants me."

"I want you!" Mother Teresa told her, and she took the girl inside the gate to Shishu Bhavan, where there was always enough room for one more child.

7

SHANTI NAGAR

ONE DAY IN 1957 FIVE LEPERS CAME TO MOTHER TERESA. "OUR FAMILIES sent us away. They are afraid they will catch our sickness. We lost our jobs and have no place to live and nothing to eat." They had been searching for food in garbage cans. Mother and her sisters washed their sores and gave them medicine, milk and rice.

Mother set up a shelter at Gobra on the outskirts of Calcutta. Soon more than 150 lepers lived there.

Eight months later the government wanted this land to house other poor people. Mother Teresa was determined to save the lepers' home. She went to Dr. B.C. Roy, the chief minister of Bengal, a medical doctor who had taken care of Prime Minister Nehru, the king of Nepal and Mohandas Gandhi. Dr. Roy gave one hour of free medical care to poor people each morning in his own home.

Mother Teresa first met him shortly after she began her work in Calcutta. She went to his house and his secretary invited her to sit on a wooden bench. Dr. Roy entered and examined each patient's face, eyes and tongue. He spent a few minutes with each, decided what medicine each needed and what to do. When the doctor came to Mother Teresa, she said, "I didn't come for myself. Can you help us get water for the people at Motijihl?"

Dr. Roy immediately wrote a letter to the Calcutta water department. Mother kept returning to the doctor to help poor people.

One day Dr. Roy said, "Mother Teresa, call my office any time."

Now Mother Teresa needed help saving the lepers' home at Gobra. "Dr. Roy," she pleaded, "they have no place else to go."

Dr. Roy shook his head sadly. "Mother, Calcutta is overcrowded. We can't let 150 lepers get in the way of other poor people."

"But the lepers are not welcome anywhere. Promise me you won't make them leave until we've found them a place."

"What about the Bankura district?" Dr. Roy suggested.

Mother gasped. "The Bankura district doesn't even have water. Leprosy patients have to have enough water."

"We'll find them a place," Dr. Roy promised.

Although Mother Teresa could not prevent the government from transferring the lepers to another location, she delayed the move until they made adequate installations available.

To draw attention to the lepers' problems, Mother Teresa and her helpers organized street collections with cans that read: "Touch a leper with your compassion." The whole city moved to change the plight of the lepers.

When someone told Mother Teresa, "I wouldn't touch a leper for a million dollars," she replied, "Neither would I, but I would gladly do so for the love of God."

On his eightieth birthday, reporters asked Dr. Roy, "How do you feel being chief minister at the age of eighty?"

He said, "As I climbed the steps this morning, I thought of Mother Teresa, who devotes her life to the poor." The next day Mother Teresa was a superstar in Calcutta.

Although publicity brought women to join her order, more helpers, money and supplies, Mother Teresa hated being in the public eye.

She learned that new drugs could arrest leprosy if discovered in time and relieve suffering in advanced stages. Until then leprosy had been treated only in hospitals that handled a few hundred people. Lepers were reluctant to go to these hospitals because everyone would know they had the disease. The new drugs allowed patients to live at home and receive regular treatments.

When a businessman discovered the early signs, his wife said, "You must leave home so our two daughters can get husbands."

He left and was planning suicide until the sisters gave him the new drugs. He was cured and became one of Mother's helpers.

"There are risks of infection involved in touching them," Mother said, "but we must take risks to help them." The sisters were willing to tend the lepers' wounds, but some asked, "How will we know if we have the disease?"

"Speak with the doctors," Mother said, "and do whatever they tell you."

The doctors said, "Do not touch any contagious patient."

"What should I do?" asked a sister tending an old woman in the latest stages.

"Do not run from the danger," Mother said, "but obey the doctor and you can help the patients for a longer time."

Originally, Mother planned to set up leprosy clinics in seven districts. One was in Motijihl, but a businessman turned some congressmen against the clinics, so Mother got the idea for mobile clinics. "We shall go to leper colonies with ambulances, giving advice, medicine and Christian love."

She thanked the businessman who fought the clinics. "You have made our job easier by inspiring us to use mobile clinics."

During the next two months an electric company donated ten thousand rupees. A Hindu specialist in leprosy, Dr. Sen, offered his services exclusively to Mother.

In 1956 Catholic Relief Services gave Mother a van for her mother and child mobile clinics. On September 1, 1957, Archbishop Perier opened Mother's first mobile clinic at the

Calcutta children's home. The mobile van visited four bustees each week: Motijihl, Howrah, Dappa and Tiljala.

There was still a need for hospitals and villages for lepers who were contagious or unable to care for themselves. Mother Teresa wanted to build small villages where they could live, work and raise their children.

Barrackpore was a village with paper mills, jute mills and rows of shanties where 250 homeless lepers lived. The local Methodist minister donated some land. The Anglican bishop offered financial assistance. And Mother Teresa obtained more land from the city.

Mother Teresa and Ann Blaikie found a site for a leper clinic but an angry crowd gathered. A village official asked, "Do you want a leper clinic here?" The people shouted, "No!" They threw stones at Mother and Ann. The two women ran to their car ducking the stones.

"I don't think God wants a clinic here," Mother said. "We must pray and find out where he wants it."

In March 1959 the first permanent leprosy clinic, Titagarh, was opened for those who were contagious or in the last stages.

At the clinic the lepers received their medicines and learned to weave their own bandages, make shoes from foam rubber and old tires, sew their own clothing and do simple carpentry. They even built their own houses.

One problem was lack of money for medicine. The lepers' healthy children would become lepers if they did not receive the drugs in time.

In Calcutta not one hospital specialized in leprosy even though over forty thousand lepers lived there.

Mother Teresa's dream to build a home for lepers came true when Shanti Nagar ("the City of Peace") was built in Asansol. The government donated thirty-four acres of land, and the sisters and lepers planted trees, cared for flower gardens and stocked ponds with fish. Volunteers taught the lepers to make bricks and build their own cottages.

The seriously ill had comfortable wards while families lived in cottages. When their disease was arrested, parents lived with their children. A nursery held children born at Shanti Nagar whose parents were contagious. People suggested the children be removed from the town, but Mother refused. "How can people deprived of everything give up their children, and how can innocent children be snatched from their parents?"

Lepers planted rice and wheat, raised cattle and chickens, wove baskets and started their own printing press. They had community kitchens, workshops and a school. They no longer had to beg.

Mother put Sister Francis Xavier Orzes, a medical doctor, in charge of the City of Peace. A few years younger than Mother Teresa, Sister Francis Xavier was also born in Yugoslavia and had been a Sister of Loreto. She was cheerful and energetic and kept Shanti Nagar well-scrubbed, comfortable and pleasant. She used flowers and bright colors to keep the community cheerful.

Some lepers had trouble with the police. Sajada, a middle-aged man who had been in prison for murder, hung around Shanti Nagar awhile and then disappeared for months. The sisters begged him, "Please come for your medicine." When the pain got bad, he came for treatments. When he felt better, he went off to drink. One day he was in such pain that he took a knife and cut off a sore and almost bled to death. When he drank, he became angry, cursed loudly, started fights and ended up in jail.

One morning when Mother Teresa came to visit Shanti Nagar, Sister Francis Xavier asked her, "May I speak with you alone, Mother?"

"Of course, sister."

They went to the sacristy of the chapel.

"I have leprosy, Mother," Sister Francis said calmly. "Several of us sisters have been diagnosed."

"Let's pray and turn the situation over to Our Lord," Mother said. Sister Francis said, "Mother, I'm sorry we did not follow Dr. Sen's rules not to touch those with contagious wounds. But when you see Jesus in his distressing disguise and you know he gladly died for you, how can you put your own health before caring for him?"

"I know, sister," Mother Teresa said. "I never told you not to touch them. I told you to listen to the doctors carefully so you understand the situation. Would you like to come to the Motherhouse in Calcutta until you are healed?"

"No, thank you, Mother Teresa. We have discussed this and have decided to remain here with our lepers." They refused any special care or hospital.

All the sisters were cured as the disease was caught early and treated with the new powerful drugs. Sister Francis remained in charge of Shanti Nagar.

8

Rome Via Las Vegas

In 1960 Mother Teresa left India for the first time in thirty-one years to go to Las Vegas to speak to the National Council of Catholic Women. Mother asked, "Wonder why they want me? Surely they can find a speaker closer to them."

Mother called Archbishop Peder for his advice. "Mother, you should definitely speak to those Catholic women in America."

"Speaking to a large crowd terrifies me," Mother said.

"Trust the Holy Spirit to handle the speech."

"Oh, your Grace, the Holy Spirit handles everything I do. But I still feel nervous whenever I speak."

On a brisk October day Mother Teresa flew to Las Vegas alone. She wondered why people laughed when she asked for a ticket to Las Vegas.

She was told, "Las Vegas is known for its gambling, drinking and quick marriages after Reno divorces. There aren't too many nuns who travel great distances to come here."

"It sounds like a good place for a meeting of Catholic women," Mother said.

Inside the banquet room over three thousand women examined Mother Teresa's cheap white cotton sari and her simple sandals. They had never seen a Catholic nun dressed that way.

Mother sat saying her rosary as a well-dressed woman described her work in Calcutta and then introduced her. Mother placed her hands together palm to palm and bowed her head. "This is the way we greet people in India. This is my first time to speak in public."

When Mother Teresa spoke of her people and the work they did, she relaxed and spoke enthusiastically of God's love.

The audience visualized the poor in India, just as Mother did when she was a little girl listening to the missionary.

"We depend completely on God's providence. We go to Hindus, Muslims and Christians and tell them, 'I have come to give you a chance to do something beautiful for God.'"

The women stood and applauded. She put her hands together once more and bowed, then returned to her seat.

Without a word, the women put money into the big bag of army cloth Mother carried.

While the convention was going on, the entertainment and gambling continued. On her way from the convent where she stayed, Mother looked at the electric signs, the nightclubs, the flashing lights.

"What do you think of Las Vegas, Mother?" asked a woman.

"It reminds me of the Hindu Festival of Lights," she said.

On the way back to Calcutta, Mother took her constitution to Rome for the pope's approval. If the Missionaries of Charity became a society of pontifical right, they could work anywhere in the world. After she fastened her seatbelt, Mother said the rosary. After three rosaries she read a few chapters of her prayer book and fell asleep.

When the plane landed in Rome, Mother tried to control her excitement. Rome, the Eternal City, home of the Vatican, has been a place of pilgrimage for Catholics for many centuries. Saint Peter was crucified here. Many great saints such as Agnes, Sebastian and Cecilia were buried in the catacombs.

Besides seeing Rome for the first time, she would see her beloved brother Lazar after thirty years.

Lazar was now fifty-three years old. He had been living in Palermo, Italy, for many years. His wife and daughter were with him.

Lazar threw his arms around Mother. "I guess I was wrong when I said you were burying yourself," he laughed. "This is my wife, Maria. She is the heroine who threw herself on top of me when Albanian partisans tried to kill me."

Mother Teresa squeezed Maria's hand. "Thank you for loving my Lazar. Thank you for saving his life."

Maria smiled. "The would-be killers changed their minds, thank God," she said.

"And this is our daughter, Agi. She's ten years old."

Mother hugged her niece.

"If only our mother and Aga could be here," Lazar said.

Mother said, "It's been so long since we had news from them."

In 1932 Lazar arranged for his sister Aga to join him in Tirana, Albania. Aga worked as a translator and later as a broadcaster for Radio Tirana. In 1934 Lazar and Aga convinced their mother to sell her home in Skopje and live with them in Albania. The three of them lived together until Lazar left to fight in the Second World War.

Several men asked for Aga's hand in marriage, but she wanted to care for her mother.

Both Mother Teresa and Lazar kept in touch with their mother, Drana, and Aga until the Marxist regime cut off all communication. "I contacted everyone I could think of," Lazar said, "trying to bring them to Italy. Finally, I got a letter from Aga. They were lonely and sad, but they were healthy. We will keep praying, and I will keep working with my friends from the embassy."

"Yes," Mother Teresa said. "God willing, we will all be together one day soon."

Pope John XXIII invited Mother to a Mass in the Sistine Chapel under Michelangelo's frescoes of creation and the last judgment. She said, "Now I can carry all my Missionaries to the feet of Christ's vicar and obtain for them the graces they need to become saints."

As the pope left the chapel, Mother was the only one to kiss his ring. He gave her his blessing.

Mother took her papers to the Sacred Congregation for the Propagation of the Faith. She said her rosary while the cardinal and the archbishop bent over the papers she had given them. They asked Mother Teresa many questions. "What kind of work do the sisters do? What training have they had? What is this fourth vow?"

The cardinal said, "I don't understand how you expect to work in a mission land without a regular source of income."

"We put our trust completely in the Lord," Mother said. "He has never deserted us. Of course, our sisters have few material needs since we live a life of poverty in dress and housing. We don't want to have more than the poor who live around us."

The men examined the sisters' prayer book. It was printed in English on inexpensive paper. The archbishop said, "This book has no formal permission."

"They are poor," the cardinal explained.

Now that her mission was completed, Lazar took her to the Rome airport to return to Calcutta. "I will continue to try to get Mother and Aga out of Albania," he promised.

"My prayers will be with you. Take good care of your family," Mother told her brother.

"And you take good care of yours," Lazar said.

9

BRANCHING OUT

IN THE AUTUMN OF 1962, POPE JOHN XXIII SUMMONED ALL BISHOPS TO Rome for the Second Vatican Council. At a coffee bar underneath St. Peter's, Archbishop Fonturvel Benitez of Barquisimeto, Venezuela, talked with the papal internuncio to New Delhi, Archbishop James Robert Knox, about the lack of priests and religious in South America. Their conversation continued for days and helped bring the Missionaries of Charity to the new world.

Archbishop Knox told Archbishop Benitez about Mother Teresa's order. "Yes, that is exactly what my diocese needs!"

In the fall of 1964 Mother Teresa visited Venezuela. Her escorts, Father Tomas and Father Manuel, showed Mother Teresa around the country. Lovely jacarandas were in bloom everywhere. "There are only three priests who serve thirty-five communities," the priests explained.

They took her to the jungle where people lived in houses built of mud and bamboo. Half-naked children stared at Mother and her companions. "This is Mother Teresa," Father Tomas said. "She wants to bring some sisters to help you."

In the city of Cocorote they went to the small Spanish church dedicated to Saint Jeronimo. "One of us says Mass here regularly," Father Tomas said.

"Then our sisters will come here," Mother said. "I put their spiritual care in your hands."

On May 2, 1965, the pope recognized the Missionaries of Charity as a society of pontifical right, allowing them to work outside of India.

When the sisters applied for passports and visas for Venezuela, there was much excitement in the government offices of India. "We have always been the country that received missionaries," a secretary said.

Mother said, "India is now the country that sends the missionaries."

A year after her first visit to Venezuela, she sent four sisters to Cocorote. Within months she sent three more. The original group was all Indian: Sister Nirmala, Sister Pauline, Sister Justin, Sister Rosario, Sister Paul and Sister Dolores.

The bishop and the local people had prepared a luxurious home for the sisters, but Mother had them give everything away. The neighbors made dresses and bedspreads out of the drapes. The family that received the refrigerator did not have electricity, so they put the new appliance on its back, filled it with ice from a friend's refrigerator and had an old-fashioned ice box.

The rectory of the little church became their convent. There was a bare wooden table and several simple chairs. Someone donated a station wagon and taught the sisters how to drive. They painted it a bright blue and drove to all the isolated villages.

The sisters taught sewing, typing and English. They became a bridge between the rich and the poor. A butcher donated meat and stewing chickens. A poor man with a small business donated a few tortillas every day. The sisters helped the priests prepare the children for their First Communion. The children called the sisters "our sisters" because their skin was dark like the children's.

Someone offered the sisters a site for a community center, a city block with the ruins of an old hotel. It had become the town garbage dump with weeds everywhere.

When Mother Teresa and the sisters arrived, some men shouted, "Don't walk in the grass! There are snakes!" The sisters looked worried, but Mother said, "Let's get the people to help us clean the space." The local people cleared out the dump, and the sisters used it as a refuge for the homeless.

"Our sisters do almost everything," Mother said. "They preach. They lead prayers. They even give Holy Communion. The only thing they can't do is celebrate the Mass."

"They can't hear confessions," someone said.

"They hear confessions all the time," Mother said. "They just can't give absolution."

Sister Leonia, a medical doctor who was in charge of the house in Raigarh, India, came to Venezuela. She was brushing her teeth when she began coughing. She made dry gagging sounds. The sisters rushed her to the hospital where she was tested immediately. "I'm sorry, but she has rabies," a doctor told the waiting sisters. Sister Leonia's eyes were shut, and he thought she was unconscious.

"What can we do?" a sister asked.

"Pray," the doctor said. "That's all any of us can do. She will be dead within forty-eight hours."

Several sisters remembered that months earlier, back in Raigarh, Sister Leonia had rescued a puppy from a pack of wild dogs and had been bitten. She had cauterized the wound, but rabies was very difficult to prevent.

Sister Leonia overheard the doctor's dire pronouncement. "There is so much work to do," she thought. "I can't die now!"

Mother Teresa and the other sisters brought her back to the house. Mother sat by her, took her hand and said, "I have received you into this work for Jesus. I will be with you when you go to him."

Sister Leonia relaxed, but then her body was overcome by terrible spasms. The sisters called the doctor, who came right away. The spasms continued, but all of Sister Leonia's attention was on Jesus as she prepared to go home to him. "I've never seen anyone with such superhuman control," the doctor said. "Most people with rabies scream. It is a horrible pain."

Mother Teresa was by her side when Sister Leonia died forty-five hours later.

While Mother was in Venezuela, she saw there was a desperate need for a house where homeless girls could wait for their babies. The governor said, "Mother Teresa, if you find a suitable location, our civil authorities will take care of the finances."

When the sisters found a site, the landowners' lawyer suggested a meeting. The governor couldn't attend this meeting, but promised to pay whatever price they agreed upon. The lawyer said, "The owner is asking five million bolivars" (approximately one million dollars). Mother shouted, "No! You do not speculate with the poor!" She refused to negotiate. In spite of this setback, Mother and her sisters were able to establish a home in Venezuela.

By 1963 Mother Teresa saw a need for a religious order of men. Several men wanted a congregation of brothers with the same spirit as the sisters. In the beginning Father Henry, Mother's friend from her days at St. Mary's, helped teach her brothers, but he did not join. On March 25, 1963, Archbishop Albert D'Souza blessed the new branch, and they began their work though they were not yet part of the official church.

In 1964 Father Ian Traves-Bell, an Australian Jesuit priest, spent a few weeks at the Calcutta children's home. He was a tall, thin, bearded young man with a warm personality, a quick smile and twinkling eyes. He saw Mother Teresa working hard all day and writing letters half the night. He watched the new brothers, so intense in their prayer and in their work. The day before he left, he and

Mother Teresa walked in the playground with the children calling Mother and tugging at her sari. "Father, have you thought about working with our poor?" Mother asked.

"I love working with the poor, but I could never give myself to them completely the way you do, Mother."

She told him, "None of us can give ourselves completely to anything unless the Lord is calling us."

Father Traves-Bell said, "I am too settled in my work." (He wrote books explaining Christianity to non-Christian readers.)

"Let's put it all in God's hands," Mother said.

"Of course, Mother," he said. "We are all in his hands."

The next day he left Calcutta with no plans of returning. In less than a year he was back in Calcutta.

"You told me of your second call, Mother. Well, I too received a call within a call. I want to give myself to Jesus in the poorest of the poor."

"Will you be my general servant for the Missionaries of Charity brothers?" Mother asked.

The Jesuits encouraged him to join Mother's brothers. He became Brother Andrew, general servant of the Missionaries of Charity brothers.

"He is a holy person," Mother said. "I am happy to put the brothers in his charge."

"What will the brothers wear?" Mother asked Brother Andrew.

"We will wear simple pants and shirts with a crucifix on the shoulder."

Mother Teresa would have preferred for the brothers to wear clothes that identified them as Missionaries of Charity, but she allowed them to make their own decisions.

"There will be some priests as well as brothers among you," she said, "so you can open houses from a church." There were fewer brothers than sisters, but their life was the same, working for the very poor and the very ill.

They ate simple food, wore plain clothes and shared whatever they had. They worked with lepers, young people with problems, sick people, homeless children and the dying. They helped people find work. They worked with boys in Mother Teresa's schools. They made homes for homeless children and helped those addicted to drugs and alcohol.

Many men wanted to join but were not emotionally or physically strong enough. Brother Andrew invited young men to "come and see" what the life was like. He called those who accepted his invitation "come and sees." Mother Teresa took over the term also for young women who wanted to experience the sister's life before making a commitment.

When Brother Andrew first joined the Missionaries of Charity brothers, there were twelve young men. They lived on the first floor of Shishu Bhavan until they found a three story house at 7 Mansatala Row, in Kidderpore, Calcutta. Their first work developed out of the Missionaries of Charity sisters' work. The brothers cared for the men in the home for the dying and for the male lepers.

One day the sisters found a crippled, mentally disabled boy playing on the streets. "What's your name?" they asked.

"My name is Johnny Walker," he said proudly.

"Where do you live?" they asked.

"Wherever I am," he said.

"Do you have any family?"

"No, I am all alone."

They took Johnny to the brothers. Johnny never learned to read or write, but he was always full of joy. He never got upset, and he made other boys forget their sadness or anger. He always had a funny song or dance. Johnny loved to pray and attend Mass. He loved God and felt that a smile and a happy voice would bring people closer to God. Johnny Walker died at the age of eighteen when he fainted in a few inches of water and drowned. Brother Andrew said, "Johnny's a saint after a joyful, successful life if ever there was one."

In November 1964 Pope Paul VI visited Bombay for a eucharistic congress. Millions of Indians lined the papal route for a glimpse of the Holy Father. Hindus believe they receive a special blessing called "darshan" in the presence of a holy person.

Mother Teresa left her sisters' house to attend the pope's welcoming ceremony, but she never arrived. On the street next to the palace where the ceremony was to take place, she found a dying couple leaning on one another, both very weak. Their faces were covered with blood and they were so thin their bones were visible. Mother held the man's hands. She said a few words of comfort, and he fell into her arms, dead. She laid him under a tree, picked up his wife and carried the woman to Bombay's House of the Dying.

Mother Teresa did not reach the opening ceremony to honor the pope's visit nor did she see Pope Paul VI in the big white Lincoln Continental that he had been given. Pope Paul VI visited the poor sections of Bombay and was deeply moved when his escort told him about Mother Teresa. "Before I leave India," he said, "I wish to do something for Mother Teresa and her poor."

Mother could not even join the crowd at the airport saying good-bye to the pope. She was in the home for the dying caring for an old man who was taking his last breaths. The pope gave his blessing to the large crowd and said, "I am donating this white motorcar to Mother Teresa, to help in her great work of love."

Mother never rode in the car. She raffled it off for a half-million rupees. A poor widow who held the winning ticket gave the car to her son, but he could not afford the gas. When they sold the car, they gave half of the money to Mother Teresa. With the money, Mother built a hospital for Shanti Nagar, the City of

Peace. She named the main street Paul VI Avenue to show her gratitude to the pope.

10

Buried in Albania

MOTHER TERESA REJOICED WHEN A SISTER HANDED HER A LETTER FROM her mother in Albania. Her hands shook as she opened the envelope and devoured the letter in her beloved mother's familiar hand. Her mother's handwriting was unsteady with sudden stops where the pen had slipped. Mother Teresa focused on the last lines of the letter: "All I ask of God is to see you and Lazar before I die."

"Please, dear Jesus, give her this last wish if it is your will, and if it isn't, comfort her with your loving presence," Mother prayed. Right away she wrote Lazar, who asked his friends at the embassy to help. They received a reply from Albania: "Mrs. Drana Bojaxhiu and Miss Aga Bojaxhiu are physically unable to travel abroad at this time."

"If one of us could go there," Lazar wrote to Mother Teresa, "I know it would be a great comfort to mother."

"You work on our going to Albania," Mother wrote, "and I shall try to get them over here."

In July 1966 Mother Teresa made another trip to Venezuela to visit her sisters and to open a house for the destitute. On her way back to Calcutta she stopped in Rome to see Lazar.

Lazar handed her a letter he had just received from their sister Aga in Albania. She wrote, "Our beloved mother is dying of loneliness. Her last wish is to see you both. I am in good health, although I too miss my brother and sister."

Lazar said, "The Albanian officials lied. They are prisoners behind the Iron Curtain. We must get them out."

Mother Teresa visited the Albanian embassy in Rome. It was in an old building that looked deserted. She rang the doorbell repeatedly. Finally a man opened the door. He looked amazed to find someone there. Mother Teresa said in her original language, "I am from Albania." The man mumbled an answer in Albanian. Mother assumed it was an invitation to enter the embassy, so she followed him inside.

Although it was the middle of the day, the hall was dark. The man flipped on the lights, and Mother Teresa saw that all the shutters were closed. She could see some overstuffed antique armchairs covered with muslin. She wondered if her mother and her sister were living in the dark back in Tirana. The man sat in an armchair and motioned for Mother Teresa to do the same.

"I am Albanian," Mother repeated. The man replied in Albanian so rapid Mother could not make out anything he said. She attempted to say something else in Albanian, but the words escaped her. She blushed. "I've forgotten my own mother tongue." Then she asked, "Do you speak Serbo-Croatian?"

"I do," he said.

"I can't find the words in my childhood tongue," she began. "That was so long ago. You see, sir, my family is Albanian. Almost forty years ago, I went to India to become a Catholic nun. That was the last time I saw my mother and my sister. Now they are living in Tirana. I was christened Agnes Gonxha Bojaxhiu, but now everyone calls me Mother Teresa." She was comfortable in Serbo-Croatian, and the man relaxed and listened to her story. He offered her coffee, but she explained the rule of her order that she was not to accept food or drink outside the convent. "Tell me about your order," he said.

"We serve the poor in the streets of Calcutta. We are Missionaries of Charity, carriers of God's love." The man inspected

Mother Teresa, noting her inexpensive sari and her bare feet in well-worn sandals. He looked puzzled. She told the man about the home for the dying and how the Missionaries of Charity gave free education to the poor. Mother Teresa said, "I come here as a little girl trying to reach her mother who is very ill."

Tears dropped from the man's eyes. He wiped his face with a white handkerchief. "You see, my mother is eighty-one and hasn't seen me since I was eighteen. I have tried everything I know to get to my mother. Only the Albanian government can give me permission to go there or give her permission to come to Rome."

"I promise to do my best," the man said. "Come back tomorrow. I will speak to the attaché."

"Thank you," Mother Teresa said. "I will be here."

The next day the attaché was waiting when Mother arrived. He spoke to her in Albanian. She was able to answer him slowly, falteringly, searching for words that she once could speak without thinking but struggled to recall. He seemed satisfied she was who she said she was. "I will get in touch with the government in Tirana and see what we can do for your mother and sister."

Later in the week Mother Teresa returned to the embassy. "I wish to speak with the attaché," she said.

"He is outside of Rome," a staff member told her.

"Have you any word about the exit visas?" Mother asked.

"We have no news of them," the man said.

"Where did the attaché go?" Mother asked.

"To Albania," the man replied. He did not invite her inside.

Mother Teresa was convinced the attaché would help her mother and sister once he got to Albania. She rushed to tell Lazar the good news. In anticipation of their arrival, Lazar and Mother Teresa found a temporary home for Drana and Aga in Rome. They sent a telegram saying they would meet them at the airport once they got their exit visas.

"You don't know how relieved I am," Lazar told Mother Teresa. He showed her an Italian newspaper. "This is what is going on in Albania. A priest was killed for baptizing a baby. He was Father Stephan Kurti, a distant relative of ours. Mosques, churches and temples have been demolished or are being used as warehouses. Can you imagine they are storing tin cans in the cathedral? Religion is outlawed. You know how our dear mother and Aga must suffer."

"Thank God we will see them soon," Mother said.

"And to think our beloved father died trying to free Albania from outside conquerors. He gave his life so that Albania would be independent. Now Albania is sovereign, and her citizens are prisoners."

"We must pray for Albania," Mother Teresa said.

"The Albanians almost killed me too," Lazar continued. "When the Americans liberated Italy, I went to an American colonel and said, 'I am a colonel of a surrendered army. I would like to work for you.' He hired me to be his jeep driver and saved my life."

"Thank God you are still alive," Mother Teresa said. "You can help me with Mother and Aga."

There was still no word from the Albanian embassy some weeks later when Mother Teresa left for Calcutta.

"Let me know when you hear anything," Mother said.

"I don't think we'll ever hear from the embassy," Lazar said, "no good news anyway."

"All in God's time," Mother Teresa said.

She couldn't know then that she and Lazar would never again see their beloved mother and sister on this earth.

11

A WORK OF LOVE

AS A SOCIETY OF PONTIFICAL RITE, THE MISSIONARIES OF CHARITY SISTERS could consider invitations from anywhere. On December 8, 1967, they opened a center in Colombo, Ceylon (now Sri Lanka).

In March 1968 Mother received a letter from Pope Paul VI. He wrote, "I want you to open a house here in Rome." With the letter were two round-trip airplane tickets from Calcutta to Rome and a check.

Mother and Sister Frederick went to Rome to examine the situation. When they landed, the pope's limousine drove them directly to the Vatican. "I am ready to open a house, Your Holiness, if there are poor people to be served," Mother told the pope. Riding through the poorer sections they saw the desperate need. Mother told the pope, "Your Holiness, God seems to have work for us just about everywhere."

On August 22, 1968, the anniversary of the opening of the House of the Dying, Nirmal Hriday, and the Feast of the Immaculate Heart of Mary, Mother Teresa brought a team of Indian sisters to open a house in Rome.

The worst slums of Rome were in the outlying sections. Many people had no water, sewage disposal or lights. But inhabitants planted flowers, and beautiful pine trees and impressive cypresses grew between the rows of shacks.

The sisters moved into a small house near San Stefano Church. The foundation in Rome became the novitiate. While Mother was in Rome, she spent time with her brother. "It is only now that I come to know you," Lazar said.

Mother Teresa laughed. "You are still a boy."

"When I read those newspaper articles about you, I wondered how you know what to say."

"The Holy Spirit gives me the words."

"What faith!" Lazar said. "Frankly, I had little faith after I left school. Enver Hoxha, one of my schoolmates, was a firm communist. Now as you know, he's the head of Albania. Most of the students were atheists. It's no wonder my faith weakened!"

Lazar went with Mother to the Rome airport. The Italian ground crew refused to load the tin cans and assorted clothing wrapped in old newspaper. Lazar was surprised when Mother Teresa and her sisters knelt down and prayed right in the middle of customs. Finally officials agreed to take the bundles aboard.

"What were you doing?" Lazar asked.

"We were asking God to change the officials' minds."

Mother Teresa tried to be on time for all her appointments. One day when she was going to meet an important Vatican official, she stopped to talk with an old man living alone in a tiny shack. She washed him and cleaned his home. Her driver warned her, "Mother Teresa, you will be late." She was late.

Her sisters said, "Only a very poor person could make Mother late for an appointment. The poor have top priority in her social calendar."

In March 1969 Mother Teresa came to Rome to prepare the constitution for the "International Association of Coworkers." Mother chose "Coworker" in honor of Mohandas Gandhi who called his helpers Coworkers.

Mother Teresa wanted her Coworkers to have the same spirit as the Missionaries of Charity. "I do not want an auxiliary dedicated to raising funds and supplies. I want a spiritual family united in their love for God in the poorest of the poor."

Mother Teresa called Ann Blaikie and her husband John to Rome to help write the rules for the Coworkers.

"Remember that many Coworkers aren't Christians," Mother said. "For every Christian who helped me in India, I had nine non-Christians."

They were the first lay organization of people of all faiths to be officially connected with a Roman Catholic order of nuns, priests and brothers. Although the association of Coworkers was now official, it remained informal. They used mimeographed newsletters describing the work of the sisters, brothers and Coworkers to keep in touch with one another. Coworkers were asked to pray daily in union with the Missionaries of Charity the following prayer:

> Make us worthy, Lord, to serve our fellow men throughout the
> world who live and die in poverty and hunger.
> Give them, through our hands, this day their daily bread, and
> by our understanding love, give peace and joy.
> Lord, make me a channel of Thy peace,
> That where there is hatred, I may bring love;
> That where there is wrong, I may bring the spirit of forgive-
> ness; that where there is discord, I may bring harmony;
> That where there is error, I may bring truth;
> That where there is doubt, I may bring faith;
> That where there is despair, I may bring hope;
> That where there are shadows, I may bring light;
> That where there is sadness, I may bring joy.
> Lord, grant that I may seek rather to comfort, than to be com-
> forted, to understand, than to be understood;
> To love rather than be loved;
> For it is by forgetting self that one finds;
> It is by dying that one awakens to eternal life.

Mother asked that all meetings begin with prayer and that once a month Coworkers unite for an hour of prayer.

Ann Blaikie was named "International Link" after Mother Teresa and Sister Frederick. Jacqueline de Decker, who had helped Mother Teresa form the Sick and Suffering Links, was named International Link for the Sick and Suffering Coworkers. Mother said, "We must pray for the work. Do it for Jesus, to Jesus and through Jesus. By being faithful to our family, to the work God gives us, we help bring souls to him. It is not how much we do that matters, but how much love we put into what we do."

Later in 1969 Archbishop James Robert Knox of Melbourne, Australia, was concerned about the native people of his country. After visiting an aboriginal reserve in New South Wales, Mother Teresa agreed to bring her sisters there. A few days before she left for Australia, Mother fell off her cot and broke her arm.

With her arm in a cast, she and the sisters opened their house in the small town of Bourke, populated by aborigines. It soon became a community center, where the sisters taught classes in cooking and sewing.

They also taught religious education to Catholic children and tutored any child who asked for help. Many poor people lived near the convent in huts of corrugated iron. Some had rust patches, and others were painted bright green or yellow.

The sisters obtained a large van and a sister drove the children from the camp to the public school.

In Melbourne Mother and five sisters found a neglected house with a leaking roof and a dirty floor. The Australian Coworkers helped clean the front room and prepared to celebrate Mass there. Since there were only five beds, one sister slept under the table. The sisters put blankets on one side of Mother to protect her broken arm. They all slept soundly, and the next morning they found that

Mother had spread all the blankets over them to keep them warm during the cold night.

Although the sisters usually found homeless people everywhere, they found no one living on the streets here. "Knock on doors asking for ill people or others with immediate needs," Mother said. The biggest challenge was dealing with those addicted to drugs or alcohol and the lonely. "If you do not bring Christ to these people, you will be wasting your time and theirs."

12

SOMETHING BEAUTIFUL FOR GOD

MOTHER TERESA MET JOURNALIST MALCOLM MUGGERIDGE IN 1968 when he interviewed her for the BBC. She arrived late, and he was impatient. They began the television interview right after she entered the room. She held her rosary throughout the interview. Malcolm was not impressed by her simple answers. The producers thought the interview was so poor that they showed it on a Sunday evening. But the studio was flooded with letters and money for Mother's work. A second showing brought in even more letters and offerings. Malcolm made a documentary film about Mother Teresa and wrote a book, both titled *Something Beautiful for God.*

Malcolm was an agnostic who had recently written a book called *Jesus Rediscovered.* Mother was convinced that he would be happy if he joined the Catholic church, but he was not interested in institutional religion. They often went to Mass together and Malcolm admitted, "I envy the peace and joy Catholics seem to feel upon receiving the Eucharist, but I can't accept all that goes with it."

"If it is his will, it will happen," Mother told him. "I will keep praying for you."

He laughed. "I hate to see you wasting all those prayers on me."

"Prayers are never wasted," she assured him. "Our Lord knows how to use them most proficiently."

Mother Teresa received many awards and honors, but she especially appreciated the Pope John XXIII Peace Prize. On January 6, 1971, Mother and her sisters rode the city bus to the Vatican where Mother was to receive her award. All of the sisters had tickets to the ceremony, but Mother had given hers to a sister who had none. At the gate, a guard stopped Mother and said, "I'm sorry, you cannot enter without a ticket." She did not know what to do. Just then a bishop stopped to congratulate Mother on being awarded the peace prize. When the sisters explained their problem to him, he told the guards, who asked for her forgiveness.

Mother Teresa's brother, Lazar, was there with his wife, Maria, and their daughter, Agi.

In presenting the award, Pope Paul VI said, "Humble Mother Teresa, in whom we see the thousands and thousands of people dedicated to the service of the most needy, becomes an example and symbol of the discovery, in which lies the secret of world peace." The twenty-five thousand dollars she received was used for the City of Peace Leprosy Foundation at Raigahr.

In the spring of 1971 West Pakistani troops invaded East Pakistan. About 250,000 refugees from East Pakistan flooded into Calcutta. Divided by culture, ethnic origin and language, citizens of West and East Pakistan could no longer be united by their common religion, Islam.

Mother Teresa and her Missionaries cared for the most helpless victims: the children, the sick, the elderly and the wounded. Mother flew to Rome where there was a conference of Catholic congregations. She described the people's agony, and fifteen sisters from various congregations returned with Mother to help the refugees. Many of the refugees lived in the sewer pipes at Salt Lake. Black, bloated corpses lay in open fields. Mother and her sisters cleaned the hospital tents for those with dysentery, cholera, smallpox and other deadly diseases. The whole world responded with food, medicine, tents, building materials, trucks and volunteers.

In December 1971 the Indian army entered East Pakistan, and on December 16 the troops of West Pakistan surrendered. East Pakistan declared its independence and changed its name to Bangladesh. Mother Teresa and her sisters were on one of the first truck convoys to enter Bangladesh after the two-week war ended. They buried the dead. In one town the authorities offered Mother and her sisters a building. Mother said, "People feel more at home if we work in smaller, plainer houses."

An estimated two hundred thousand women had been raped. As a result, many young girls were pregnant. In their culture a woman who had been raped would never find a husband, and they saw their lives as ruined. Some committed suicide.

Mother Teresa opened a house for these women in the city of Dacca. Sheikh Majuibur Rahman, leader of the new nation, said, "The women violated by the enemy should be considered national heroines." Many of the women wanted abortions. Mother begged them to have the babies and give them to her. "The sisters will take care of you, and we will find a good home for the babies."

Mother wanted to open a house in New York City early in 1971, but problems in Bangladesh kept her occupied. Finally in September five Indian sisters arrived at Kennedy airport with their bedrolls and cardboard boxes of kitchen utensils.

The Handmaids of Mary in Harlem arranged sleeping quarters for the five sisters. When Mother arrived on October 14, her sisters rushed under the ropes to greet her Indian style with a crepe paper wreath they had made. Mother gave each sister her blessing.

Mother was called to Washington, D.C., to receive an award from the Joseph P. Kennedy, Jr., Foundation. At the conference Mother Teresa watched a movie where a newborn baby with Down syndrome was allowed to starve to death. When the film ended, Mother exclaimed, "Court order or no court order, I would have snatched up that baby and run with him to a safe place where he could be saved. I wouldn't care if the police came after me. I wouldn't give up that baby."

Senator Edward Kennedy presented Mother Teresa with the award, twelve thousand dollars, a Waterford crystal vase and a crystal plate with an image of the archangel Raphael with a note: "Seraph Raphael, chief of the guardian angels who protect and guide mankind."

Rose Kennedy made a personal gift to increase Mother's award from twelve to fifteen thousand dollars. Mother gave the Waterford crystal vase to Sister Andrea, saying, "This will help turn the Dum Dum refugee center into a permanent center for retarded and handicapped children. I will call it the Nirmala Kennedy Center."

That evening Mother Teresa met Andrew Young, a man who had worked with Dr. Martin Luther King, Jr., in his nonviolent campaigns. He told Mother how Dr. King's work was inspired by Jesus and by Gandhi. Mother invited him to visit her and the sisters in Harlem. The next evening Andrew Young came to the Harlem convent. Mother Teresa asked him, "Please tell me about the beautiful things in the lives of American blacks."

"Well, Mother Teresa, religion plays an important part in the lives of southern black people. We love to sing and praise the Lord as part of our worship."

"Could you sing a hymn for me?" Mother asked. His deep, rich voice belted out "Lead, Kindly Light," one of Gandhi's favorite songs. Mother's clear soprano joined in.

Not long after that Andrew Young became the first black congressman from Georgia, then United States ambassador to the United Nations and then mayor of Atlanta.

The sisters found their own place in the South Bronx and moved out of the Handmaids of Mary's convent. "You can use the convent temporarily, Mother," a workman told her, "but all of the remaining buildings on this block are scheduled for demolition." Mother learned that many had been destroyed by arsonists and those that remained seemed ready to collapse on their own.

The American edition of *Something Beautiful for God* was published in October 1971. Author Malcolm Muggeridge and Mother Teresa appeared on *The David Frost Show, Today* (where Barbara Walters interviewed them) and several other television shows.

Mother believed that when she appeared in public it was a chance to save souls. When she agreed to receive awards and make speeches, she hoped to raise awareness about the poor. She never depended on the world's wealth to care for her poor. She wanted the rich to meet the poor, to see their beauty and learn that dignity and honor do not come from riches, but from love, forgiveness and compassion.

Senator Edward Kennedy went with Mother to the Salt Lake and the center near the Dum Dum airport in Calcutta. He said, "Most difficult of all; you see the corpse of the child who died the night before. I have a collection of personal observations that really burned my soul."

Jerry Brown, former governor of California, spent three weeks helping Mother in Calcutta. Mother said, "It is easier for me to clean a leper's wounds than to appear in public. So I made an agreement with the Lord. Each time I appear in public one soul is released from purgatory."

Later, when Mother received the Nobel Peace Prize, a Coworker said, "Well, Mother, it looks like you've cleaned out purgatory."

Mother laughed. "It doesn't take purgatory long to fill up again."

In 1972 Mother Teresa received a telegram from her brother Lazar: "Pray for Mother who died on July 12th."

Lazar and Mother Teresa had tried every way to get their mother and sister out of Albania. President John F. Kennedy,

French President Charles de Gaulle, Secretary General of the United Nations U Thant, Indira Gandhi and others had tried to help, but none of them could open the Iron Curtain long enough to allow a brief visit.

Later Mother Teresa learned that even if she'd obtained a visa there was a chance she would have not been allowed to leave Albania as long as it remained communist. Mother would have been torn between her desire to see her beloved family and her call to serve Jesus in the world. In the end, as much as it tortured her, she put her mother and sister in God's hands and stayed outside, continuing her work. She told Lazar, "Up until now I have obtained everything with love and prayer. But there are still barriers that not even love can break down. All she ever wanted was to see us once more."

Mother spent the afternoon praying. Later she said, "She is his more than mine. Our sacrifice, hers and mine, of not seeing each other has obtained much strength for the work and has brought us closer to God."

Her sister Aga was now alone in Albania. She had given up marriage to take care of her mother; now she herself was ill and there was no one to care for her. She died in Tirana on August 25, 1973.

Mother Teresa, who helped those in need all over the world, was unable to help her own family.

13

Globalization

In 1971, HOPING TO IMPROVE RELATIONS BETWEEN CATHOLICS AND Protestants, Mother and four sisters arrived in war-torn Belfast with bedrolls and a violin. They moved into a house where a priest had recently been murdered.

Northern Ireland had been a hotbed of violence for years as an underprivileged Catholic minority struggled with the Protestant majority for equal rights. The outlawed Irish Republican Army sought to gain independence from Great Britain, whose troops were ever-present. Bombings in neighborhood pubs killed hundreds.

"This is the most dangerous part of the country," one Coworker told Mother.

"That's why we are needed here."

The sisters helped widows whose husbands had been killed in the fighting, mothers who had lost sons and often husbands, too. Many were left alone with little ones.

"The Irish always believed in the sacredness of life," Mother said. "And they love the rosary and gave the world many missionaries. Many years ago I came from Yugoslavia to the Sisters of Loreto, in Rathfarnham, Ireland. My connection and my gratitude to the Irish people spring from that."

Mother wanted her sisters to work with some Anglican nuns, but she soon realized her sisters were not wanted. She was sad upon leaving Belfast, but she had requests to open houses everywhere. Because of a great drought, she went to Ethiopia to help starving people. She also went to Gaza in Israel where in 1973 displaced Palestinians and Israeli Jews fought over territory. Once more Mother's sisters moved into a place where a priest was murdered, and they had to clean up bloodstains. The sisters soon made friends with the children, the sick and the elderly.

The Missionaries of Charity brothers also went where they were most needed. In 1973 Brother Andrew, their servant general, brought a team of brothers to Vietnam where a civil war pitted the communist North against the American-supported South.

Right away the brothers began a House of Hospitality for widows with young children and poor women who were disowned by their families. They took in an attractive young Vietnamese woman named My Le who was homeless and single. She became a prostitute to support her three young children. When she gave up prostitution, her parents refused to help, and she became desperate for a home and food.

The little community grew until more than sixty people lived there. They were supportive of one another, and they relied on the brothers less and less.

In 1974 the brothers moved to Phnom Penh, Cambodia, where there was more need. The Khmer Rouge, a repressive communist movement, had gained control of Cambodia, and many Cambodians were murdered. Every town along a thirty-mile stretch of Highway Four through Phnom Penh had been destroyed. Most survivors were in refugee camps. The brothers opened a Hospitality House for the refugees, and when their first house was full, they opened a second.

By 1975 the war was accelerating each day, and Brother Andrew felt the situation was too dangerous for the young brothers. No one wanted to leave, but they had taken a vow of obedience. Only Brother Brian Walsh, a twenty-three-year-old American, refused to go. Two brothers considered taking him with them by force, but Brother Brian was last seen with some French Benedictine monks. The brothers got out just in time, for the Khmer Rouge occupied Phnom Penh and soon North Vietnam took over Saigon.

When everyone was evacuated except for Brother Brian, Brother Andrew decided to stay. He went from one Hospitality House to the next doing whatever he could. Soon the Khmer Rouge took over all the houses, and the people were homeless once more. Each day a new list of foreigners to be deported was posted, and at last Brother Andrew's name was on it. "I shall never be the same, and I shall have an ache in my heart for these people until I die."

Two million people perished in Cambodia. Brother Brian was presumed dead. Many brothers wrote to Brian's mother. She shared her son's last letter: "I hope you are at peace. Even if this is wrong, staying on here, I know that God can make it up to you a hundred times over. I don't believe I'm doing anything wrong. But I have a lot of peace that I know belongs to you as much as it does to me. We must think of the words: 'There is no greater love than to lay down one's life for one's friends.'"

In June 1975 Mother Teresa represented the Vatican at the World Conference of the International Women's Year held on the thirtieth anniversary of the United Nations in Mexico City. Mother Teresa introduced the pope's resolution, that poverty limits basic human rights and creates powerlessness. President Echeverria of Mexico invited Mother Teresa to his home. He asked, "What is the meaning of this sari you wear?"

"I chose it because it was the way poor women in India dress," she said. "We wear it at all times." She explained that the

Missionaries of Charity sisters were Catholic nuns in the traditional sense.

Then he said, "Mother, I would like you to bring your sisters to Mexico. I will see that they get everything they need."

The president's wife introduced some of their eight children to Mother Teresa and handed her a small cross. "This as an example of the fine work done by our poor people."

The following year Mother's sisters arrived in Mexico City. President Echeverria gave them a vehicle. Mother and her sisters chose a simple hut by the city dump as their home.

By October 1975 Mother Teresa was back in Calcutta to celebrate the twenty-fifth anniversary of the Missionaries of Charity. She asked the people of Calcutta to help her give thanks with prayer services in their own denominations. She received responses from the Hindus, Buddhists, Catholics, Muslims, Jains, Jews, Sikhs, Armenians, Assemblies of God and the Methodist and Mar Thomas Syrian churches. Mother Teresa recited the Magnificat, Mary's prayer, in the Moghen David Synagogue. "For he that is mighty hath done great things to me; And holy is his name. He hath filled the hungry with good things; and the rich he hath sent empty away."

Mother took different sisters and third year novices to each religious celebration. It may have been a historical first, so many spiritual paths united together in thanksgiving.

From their small beginning of twelve Missionaries of Charity, the group now had 1,133 members living all around the world. In India they had houses in Calcutta, Andhra Pradesh, Bihar, Gujarat, Haryana, Kerala, Meghalaya, Madhya Pradesh, Maharashtra, Mysore, Orissa, Tamil Nadu, Uttar Pradesh, Union Territories and West Bengal. Outside India were houses in Africa, Australia, Bangladesh, Europe, Mauritius, the Middle East, Papua New Guinea, the United States and South America.

At the Jain temple Mother Teresa and her sisters sat near Jain nuns in white saris. In the far corner sat Jain monks who wore no clothes, had no possessions, practiced celibacy, fasting and mortification. Mother Teresa was moved by a Jain nun whose head was covered with blood as she pulled out her hair one strand at a time as a penance. Mother reached under her veil and pulled out some of her own hair to feel in union with the nun.

October 2 was the birthday of the late Mohandas Gandhi. Mother Teresa was glad to include his memory in the Silver Jubilee celebration. The Leprosy Center at Titagarh, which had been run by the sisters, was turned over to the Missionaries of Charity brothers and renamed Gandhiji Prem Nivas (Gandhi Center of Love).

On October 4 Mother and her sisters went to the Hindu temple of Shree Lakshmi Narayan. Everyone touched Mother's feet. The priest and all present invoked the thousand names of God with great devotion in solemn Sanskrit.

When October 7 arrived, Mother was surrounded by most of the women who had joined her twenty-five years earlier. Sisters Agnes, Dorothy, Margaret Mary, Bernard, Florence, Clare and Francesca were there. Sister Gertrude was in Yemen and Sister Laetitia in Papua New Guinea. The Mass was celebrated by Archbishop Picachy with those priests who had served as chaplains to the sisters. Among them were Father Edward Le Joly and Father Celest Van Exem. Father Julian Henry said he did not like public ceremonies and promised to thank God in private.

Michael Gomes, Mother's original landlord, served the Mass. His wife, Agnes, and daughter Mabel, who had often gone with Mother Teresa into the slums, were there also. Brother Andrew was present with some of the brothers. In the front row were some survivors from the House of the Dying. The sisters called them "our most precious gift."

Later that week Michael Gomes was astonished when he opened the door and found Mother Teresa standing there. "I want you and your family to have this," Mother said, handing him the beautiful picture of Our Lady that had hung over the altar in the upper room.

A week later Mother Teresa went to New York to join their celebration of the United Nations' anniversary. The other speakers represented Buddhism, Judaism, Islam and Hinduism.

When she left New York, Mother was whisked off to Washington, D.C., to speak on peace at a sequel to the International Women's Year conference. Margaret Mead spoke on equality. When she was introduced to Mother Teresa, she kissed Mother's hand. Dr. Elisabeth Kübler-Ross, who had written a best-selling book, *Death and Dying,* after years of working with dying patients, wanted to meet Mother Teresa. They shared their experiences and their recognition of the need for personal loving care for the dying. Mother explained to Dr. Kübler-Ross that most of the people who died at her home for the dying in Calcutta were Hindu or Muslim. "We don't try to convert them to Christianity but to bring them closer to God. We say we are giving them a ticket to Saint Peter, and they all like that."

Kübler-Ross told Mother Teresa, "Most of my work has been to help the dying person feel a part of the living so that they are not isolated and lonely. The impersonality of modern hospitals has led me to recommend the hospice movement for the dying. They need a loving, supportive environment where pain is controlled or prevented along with unpleasant symptoms."

"Yes," Mother agreed. "My prayer is that before they die, all people know that they are loved."

14

The Contemplatives

On September 8, to celebrate Our Lady's birthday, Sister Nirmala took her contemplative sisters to Crotona Park. They were praying when a young man in a black suit shouted, "Jeremiah said that God will pour out his anger and blood will flow on the earth."

Sister Nirmala quoted the prince of peace.

"I am preparing for war!" the man shouted. "I am an instrument of destruction."

"What is your name?" Sister Nirmala asked.

"My name is Hassan."

"Hassan means 'good,' " Sister Nirmala said. "You can't be an instrument of destruction with that name."

Hassan pointed a switchblade at Sister Nirmala's throat. She held up her cross and her rosary. "These are my only weapons," she said. "They mean that the lion and the lamb can live together in peace."

The other sisters gathered around. Hassan withdrew his knife and joined the sisters in their prayers and hymns. When he was leaving, he promised, "I will be the guardian angel of the park, and I will protect you here." They saw him many times after that and he greeted them joyfully.

Mother visited a Protestant brother, Roger Schutz, at his ecumenical center in Taize, France. Pope John XXIII had blessed Brother Roger for his efforts to reconcile all Christians. Mother joined him for evening prayers. Over three thousand young people crowded into the chapel to pray for peace. Both Mother Teresa and Brother Roger were saddened by the divisions among Christians. They asked God to bless all humanity with love. They became close friends and did a book together on the Way of the Cross. (On August 16, 2005, Brother Roger was on his way to evening prayer when a deranged woman stabbed him to death.)

Mother Teresa traveled the earth helping wherever people lost lives and homes. In 1976 she opened centers in six new countries. In 1977 she opened seven and in 1978 there were twenty-five new foundations, sixteen of them in India. By the end of 1979, there were 158 foundations.

On June 8, 1978, Mother opened her first house at Zagreb, Yugoslavia, Sister Mary Magdalene's hometown, where Mother Teresa said good-bye to her mother and sister before going to Ireland. Mother Teresa apologized to an Albanian priest for being unable to speak the language. He said, "Mother Teresa, you speak the language of the soul, which everyone everywhere understands."

She said, "You are right, Father. That language alone can bring us all together."

The archbishop of Zagreb told Mother Teresa that he was a Coworker and that the Coworker movement was popular in Yugoslavia.

After Zagreb Mother Teresa and Father Michael Gabric, another Coworker priest, visited Skopje, Mother's birthplace. She went to her father's grave, but a 1963 earthquake had destroyed the cemetery. Mother Teresa stared at the ground and said, "I don't know where my mother or my sister are buried. I thought I could find my father's grave. It doesn't matter. They are all together now with Jesus and his mother." She fell to her knees and spent time in silent prayer.

Her childhood home and Sacred Heart Church were also both destroyed in the quake. She made a pilgrimage to Our Lady of Letnice, where she first heard God's voice. She asked Mary to help her belong only to God and to keep her faithful. "They changed her dress," Mother said. "But her eyes and her face are the same."

In 1979 Mother took some sisters to war-ravaged Beirut. They found themselves on a street with two groups shooting at each other. They wanted to shout, "Stop shooting!" in Arabic, but they were so frightened they forgot the words. Finally Mother shouted in English, "Stop!" The firing stopped and the sisters continued down the road. They found a house and filled it with orphans and other victims of the conflict.

Mother Teresa tried to attend the openings of all her houses. The Holy Father gave her a diplomatic passport from the Vatican and since India was unaligned in the Cold War she could enter every country.

Whenever Mother could not attend an opening, she sent her sisters with a request to the church and the Coworkers: "Please protect the poverty of my sisters. That is their dowry."

Several times Coworkers prepared homes for the sisters with luxurious carpets, comfortable furniture and washers and dryers. The sisters immediately pulled up the carpets and gave the "excess" furniture, washers and dryers to the poor.

More than one convent had a long line of poor people outside when they heard the sisters were giving away washers and dryers.

Someone told mother, "You are spoiling the poor." Mother said, "Jesus lives in the poorest of the poor. It isn't possible to spoil Jesus."

15

THE NOBEL PRIZE

ON OCTOBER 16, 1979, MOTHER TERESA WENT TO THE HOME FOR THE Dying, just as she did every day when she was in Calcutta. Mother cleaned a man covered with maggots, speaking to him in Bengali. "I am thirsty," the man mumbled. He drank the water Mother gave him, smiled, said a weak "thank you" and died.

"He went home with a smile," Mother said.

At 5:30 that afternoon when she returned home, she was upset to find dozens of reporters, photographers and film-makers crowded around the motherhouse. Some had even managed to get inside, although this was strictly against regulations. Ignoring the reporters, Mother went straight to Sister Mary Agnes. "What are these people doing here, Sister?" she asked.

"Why, you've won the Nobel Peace Prize, Mother, and they've come to speak with you."

Mother gasped, and said, "Please tell them to wait outside, sister." Then she slipped into the chapel.

Many people assume that winning the Nobel Peace Prize was the crowning achievement of Mother Teresa's life. From her personal point of view, it was a tragedy. As she knelt in the chapel, Mother identified with Jesus in the Garden of Gethsemane when he prayed, "Father, if it is possible, let this cup pass from me; yet not as I will, but as you will."

All her life she had envied contemplative nuns who spent their days in prayer behind convent walls. Mother Teresa thought of Saint Thérèse of Lisieux, who never left her convent from the day she entered. Yet the Little Flower had dreamed all her brief life of being a missionary in the field and offered her prayers and sacrifices each day for the priests and religious in the missions. After her death, when the church officially declared Thérèse a saint, they made her co-patron of those missions she had longed to visit.

Mother said, "Jesus, what in the world are you up to now, having me win this prize?"

In her head Mother could hear the other Teresa, Teresa of Avila, saying to God, "If this is how you treat your friends, it's no wonder you have so few of them!"

She smiled at the private joke between the three Teresas and God. "When I was a little girl reading books about saints," she said to God, "I used to pray to you, 'Lord, make me a martyr.' What I meant was for you to allow me to die for love of you. I was not praying for a life in which I would be miserable."

She caught herself and laughed aloud. The other sisters had entered the chapel one by one. They looked up at the sound of her laughter and smiled. They had a feeling of joy and gratitude that the work was appreciated and the world was coming to know the poorest of the poor. But they recognized the strain and suffering this would put on their beloved Mother Teresa. She no longer belonged just to them and the poor. Now the whole world would claim her. "I don't deserve the prize," Mother thought. "But it is not for me. It's for the poor that I will receive the prize." Her heart filled with joy. The world was coming to see and love the poor.

"Thank you, Lord, for your gift to the poorest of the poor." She continued her private conversation with God. "Lord, you know what kind of martyrdom you need from each of us. When you asked the rich young man to sell all he had, give it to the poor and follow you, it was the hardest thing for him to do. But that was not why you asked it of him. It was what he needed to do for his own salvation. He had to free himself of his attachments so he could cling to you."

The sisters then entered the chapel and began singing a hymn of thanksgiving. Mother joined them.

Crowds gathered around the motherhouse. People from all walks of life knocked on the door. They all came to tell Mother Teresa how happy they were. Photographers and journalists begged for interviews and pictures. Mother asked the Nobel Prize Committee, "How much money do you usually spend on the reception dinner?"

"Around six thousand dollars."

"That will feed four hundred of our people for a whole year. Could you please cancel the dinner and give me the money?"

"Well, Mother Teresa, that has never been done, but I'll see what we can do."

"Thank you. God bless you."

The committee sent Mother Teresa three tickets to Oslo—one for herself, and one each for Sister Mary Agnes and Sister Mary Gertrude. The sisters wondered what kind of reception Mother would have since the banquet had always been one of the highlights of the award ceremony festivals. They wondered if people would be disappointed.

During the long flight, Mother prayed her rosary, read a spiritual book and ate a slice of bread with lettuce and tomato. She made a few notes for her acceptance speech. In some ways, this would be the most important speech she had ever made. The idea of speaking to so many people made her feel weak. "Lord, I offer it all up to you. I know you will use me to bring more souls to you."

When they landed in Oslo, it was late afternoon. The sun had already set, and the Norwegian November air was cold. Carrying all her worldly goods in her homemade cloth bag, Mother stepped out of the plane. She wore her regular thin sari with sandals and a man's navy blue sweater. The sisters had been offered coats and fur boots but had turned them down. Mother Teresa was surprised to see a long line of people holding candles. They had braved the cold night to welcome her. No other recipient in the history of the Nobel Prize had ever received such a warm welcome.

Her trip to Oslo was a festive occasion for many people, but for her it was a time of great suffering. "Mother, how do you feel about winning the Nobel Peace Prize?" a reporter asked.

"It is a drop of deliverance in an ocean of suffering," Mother said. "I am myself unworthy of the prize. I do not want it personally. But by this award the Norwegian people have recognized the existence of the poor. It is on their behalf that I have come."

Meanwhile, when word of the award reached Bengal, its chief minister Jyoti Basu, a communist, held a reception in honor of Mother Teresa. "You have long been the mother of Bengal," he said. "Now you are the mother of the world."

India's President V.V. Giri added, "Mother Teresa is among those emancipated souls who have transcended all barriers of race, religion, creed and nation."

In Oslo a thanksgiving ceremony was held in the Lutheran cathedral. Afterward a thousand people carrying lighted candles walked through the streets with Mother Teresa leading the procession. It was a clear, starry night with bitter cold air. They went to a mission hall in Oslo where some girls gave Mother Teresa a check for about three hundred dollars. "Children donated this out of their pocket money," she was told. Young people all over Norway collected money and raised over seventy thousand dollars.

"Yes, money is necessary," she told the children, "but we must increase its value by seasoning it with love."

On December 10 the king of Norway welcomed his international guests who had gathered in a palace at the University of Oslo for the Nobel Prize ceremony. From Skopje, the town where Mother Teresa was born, had come Nikola Prela, the Catholic bishop. From Palermo, Italy, had come her brother, Lazar Bojaxhiu, and his daughter. Jacqueline de Decker had come from Belgium, wearing steel braces that allowed her to move. Ann Blaikie had come from England. There were Coworkers from Sweden, Denmark, Finland, Holland, France, Switzerland, Italy, Malta and the United States.

The Nobel Committee President, John Sannes, said, "The sisters, with their serene ways, their saris, their knowledge of local languages, have come to symbolize not only the best in Christian charity, but also the best in Indian culture and civilization from Buddha to Gandhi." He added, "Mother Teresa works in the world as she finds it, in the slums of Calcutta and other towns and cities. But she makes no distinction between poor and rich people or between poor and rich countries." He ended his speech saying, "Mother Teresa deserves Nobel's Peace Prize because she promotes peace in the most fundamental manner, by her confirmation of the inviolability of human dignity."

The huge crowded hall was silent as the tiny nun walked up to the speaker's stand. She bowed to the immense audience in her traditional Indian style. President Sannes handed her the gold medal and the $190,000. Mother thanked him and smiled. She waited until he was in his seat, then spoke without notes. "Let us all thank God on this beautiful occasion, for the joy of spreading peace, the joy of loving one another and the joy of recognizing that the poorest of the poor are our brothers and sisters. Let us thank God for the opportunity that we all have today, for this gift of peace that reminds us that we have been created to live that peace, and Jesus became man to bring that Good News to the poor."

She spoke from her heart about things that mattered deeply to her. Once she began to talk about the poorest of the poor, the dying, the abandoned babies, she completely forgot her own fears and discomfort and felt grateful to God for having the chance to speak about him in the least of his people.

While she spoke, everyone in the great hall was silent. The large room was overflowing with hundreds outside in the corridors. Every one was spellbound by Mother.

"We are teaching our beggars, our leprosy patients, our slum dwellers, our people of the street natural family planning. And in Calcutta alone in six years–it is all in Calcutta–we have had 61,273 babies less from the families who would have had them because they practice this natural way of abstaining, of self-control, out of love for each other."

Mother Teresa told them about the poorest of the poor in Calcutta, the people dying in the streets, the lepers and the abandoned babies. She ended with, "And how beautiful it will be that from here the joy of life of the unborn child comes out. If you become a burning light of peace in the world, then really the Nobel Peace Prize is a gift of the Norwegian people. God bless you!"

After she finished speaking, some Swedish women who admired Mother's work with the poor asked her, "Aren't you concerned about the rights of the pregnant woman, Mother?"

"I care greatly for every human being from their conception to their last breath. Jesus said whatever we do to the least of his people, we do to him. Who could be less than the little unborn baby whose scream is silence? We must love God's children everywhere. That is all he asks of us."

After the award ceremony, there was a simple reception where the Nobel Prize committee and Mother Teresa greeted the guests in person. Mother Teresa did not eat anything at all, drinking only a glass of water.

During the reception a Coworker asked, "Mother Teresa, could we see your gold medal?" Mother couldn't remember where she had put it. Mother remained cool, saying her rosary while her friends searched. A Coworker found the medal among the stack of winter coats.

It was not the crowds she dreaded, not even when they rushed toward her, surrounding her, trying to touch the hem of her garments. They saw Christ in her just as she saw him in them. What she disliked was all the praise showered on her. Mother told her Coworkers, "Some Americans said, 'Mother, they want to canonize you.' And I told them, 'Let me die first.'"

Before she left Oslo, Mother Teresa received a phone call from Violet Collins, national link for the Coworkers in the United States. "Mother, American embassy personnel in Tehran are being held captive; could you personally intercede on their behalf and ask for their freedom?" Mother promised to visit the embassy of Iran in Rome.

Saying good-bye to her Coworkers, Mother said, "Let us in every country, wherever we are, meet God with a smile. Everywhere and in everyone a smile is the beginning of world peace."

Leaving Oslo, Mother told Sister Agnes and Sister Gertrude, "Hopefully this will be the last award ceremony I shall be called to attend. We can use the prize money for our lepers and our poor, but all these appearances are interfering with our work."

16

RAISING CONSCIOUSNESS

ON DECEMBER 13, 1979, MOTHER TERESA WENT TO THE IRANIAN embassy in Rome. America was concerned with the fate of the hostages taken when the American embassy in Iran was seized by Islamic revolutionaries led by Ayatollah Khomeini. "I have come to see you about the American hostages," Mother Teresa said. "I come as a mother who longs for her children. I am willing to go to Iran or to talk to the Ayatollah on the telephone."

"I will look into the matter," the man said.

Mother and her sisters kept praying about the hostages, but there was no response from the embassy of Iran.

While she was in Rome, Mother attended a Mass celebrated by Pope John Paul II in his private chapel. She presented her proposal for a new Coworker organization of priests. He asked, "May I be the first priest to volunteer, Mother?"

She returned to India, and learned she was the first naturalized Indian to receive the Bharat Ratna, the Jewel of India.

President Neelam Sanjiva Reddy said, "Mother Teresa embodies compassion and love of humanity as few in history have done." Prime Minister Indira Gandhi said, "To meet her is to feel utterly humble, to sense the power of tenderness and the strength of love."

Mother Teresa was raising the consciousness of the entire world, helping people realize that works of mercy, feeding the hungry, sheltering the homeless, caring for the ill, clothing the naked are truly works of peace—indeed the foundation of a peaceful world.

People everywhere asked Mother Teresa for her autograph. She wrote, "God bless you. M. Teresa M.C." A sister asked, "Don't you get tired of writing your signature, Mother?" "For me, it is praying," Mother said. "When I write 'God bless you' I pray for the person."

The Holy Father gave Mother Teresa the keys to the Primaville building, a mansion on Vatican property. "Now you have a place where every child, every homeless mother awaiting a child will be welcome."

In 1980 Mother took some sisters to Skopje, Yugoslavia, her birthplace.

In May 1981 she celebrated the fiftieth anniversary of her life as a nun with a special Mass at the Motherhouse.

On June 4, 1981, President and Mrs. Ronald Reagan invited Mother Teresa to lunch at the White House. She took Sister Priscilla and Violet Collins. Mother told the president, "Your suffering from the attempt on your life has brought you closer to Jesus and to the poor who suffer so much." Afterward, when reporters asked him what he told Mother Teresa, President Reagan said, "I listened."

Later that month when Mother Teresa was awarded the Discovery Medal at Marquette University, reporters asked, "Have you made any discoveries, Mother?"

"I am too small to discover anything. Yes, I suppose it is a discovery for some that the poorest of the poor, the rejected, the throwaways are Jesus in his disguise."

Mother Teresa had passed her seventieth birthday. Someone asked, "When will you retire, Mother?" She said, "The poor cannot retire."

Mother Teresa's brother, Lazar, died of lung cancer at his home in Italy July 3. When Mother got the news, she went into the chapel and said her rosary. Later she said, "My mother must be rejoicing now. She must have been longing for him to join her, Papa and Aga. She's with her only son whom she loved more than her life. Now it only remains for our Father to call me and the whole family will be united once more."

Some people criticized Mother Teresa for not trying to change the structures of society. One reporter felt that Mother Teresa made it too easy to dump one's guilt about poverty and homelessness by a donation without confronting the problem.

Mother always said, "Giving should not be confined to money or material goods. I want people to give their hands and their hearts."

In many interviews she explained, "We give fish to the poor instead of a fishing rod because our people are too weak from hunger, too diseased and disabled, too old or too young to fish for themselves. When they are strong enough, you give them the rod and show them how to catch fish."

Some people felt Mother should not have run homes for the sick and dying if she couldn't offer modern medical care. Perhaps they failed to realize that Mother cared for people who were too poor or too sick to be cared for in traditional medical settings. Many people would rather die surrounded by Mother Teresa's loving nuns than in a sterile hospital attached to life-support machines.

She was criticized for socializing and accepting help from people like the widow of Enver Hoxha, communist dictator of Albania (the same man who would not allow her mother and sister to leave the country), Baby Doc Duvalier, the ruthless dictator of Haiti, and several questionable businessmen, including Charles Keating.

Journalist and author Christopher Hitchens, a vocal critic of Mother Teresa, accused her of spending millions of dollars on convents rather than building new hospitals. It's safe to say he was never inside one of Mother's convents because less money was spent on them than on most of the poor huts, shacks and houses around them. In El Florido, Mexico, Mother Teresa refused washing machines and dryers for her orphanage. The sisters washed all the babies' clothes and diapers by hand with a wash board and hard soap.

Mother would shake hands with a convicted murderer, a leper or someone who saw themselves as her enemy. To her, everyone was Christ in his various masks. If one understands Mother's theology, it can be seen why she did this. She forgave everyone. She followed the Bible literally. "Love God with all your heart, all your strength, all your soul and love your neighbor as yourself." Mother didn't see borders and frontiers. She saw the world as one and she loved us all. "Judge not, lest you be judged," she said.

In 1981 and 1982 polls showed Mother Teresa was the most admired woman in the world. At the end of 1982 Mother Teresa saw a copy of the *London Times* with a photograph of an elderly man on his knees receiving the Eucharist from the hands of a priest. It was Malcolm Muggeridge, the author of *Something Beautiful for God*. Mother Teresa had prayed for Malcolm to know Jesus in the Eucharist ever since they attended Mass together more than a decade earlier. She had a difficult time understanding Malcolm's resistance to full participation in the Mass since she noticed his great devotion during the liturgy. Now, years later, Malcolm and his wife had come to know Jesus in the Blessed Sacrament. Mother Teresa rejoiced. God had indeed heard her prayers.

17

NEVER SAYING NO

IN JUNE 1982 THE FRAGILE PEACE BETWEEN LEBANON AND ISRAEL WAS
shattered when Israel charged that the Palestine Liberation
Organization (PLO) critically wounded the Israeli ambassador in
London. Israel attacked southern Lebanon, demolishing PLO
strongholds. On June 10 Israeli troops reached Beirut and forced
the PLO guerrillas from the western sector practically destroying it.

Pope John Paul II received Mother Teresa at his summer residence in the hills outside of Rome. "I want to go to Lebanon," he
said, "but the cardinals say it is impossible to arrange security. Now
I hear that you are going."

"Yes, Your Holiness, I am concerned about my sisters who are
there, and I have heard about some abandoned children."

"Mother Teresa, I want you to be my personal envoy to
Lebanon."

They knelt together in the pope's private chapel and prayed for
peace.

She said, "Pray for me, Holy Father, that I won't ruin God's
work."

"Pray for me, that I won't ruin his church," responded Pope
John Paul II.

Mother Teresa flew from Rome to Cyprus. Then she traveled to
Beirut on a seventeen-hour boat ride. She found bombing and

shelling everywhere. Although the sisters claimed to be safe, their convent was within five miles of a major target.

John de Salis, head of the Red Cross in Lebanon, told Mother Teresa, "There are some mentally ill children in a nursing home near a camp of Palestinian refugees. The building has been bombed repeatedly. All of the caretakers were killed or ran away. Those children don't have food or water and some may be wounded."

"The children can be housed with the sisters," Mother said.

"The main problem, Mother," he continued, "is that the building is on the wrong side of the Green Line and there's no way to reach them."

"We have to evacuate those children," Mother said. "I will cross the line."

The guards at the Green Line checkpoint said, "You cannot go in there, Mother Teresa. There is a war going on."

"What if there is a ceasefire?" Mother Teresa asked.

"Listen to those bombs, Mother. Does that sound like a ceasefire?"

"We are praying for a ceasefire," Mother Teresa said, "and tomorrow is a feast day of the Blessed Mother. We asked her for a ceasefire to celebrate her day."

"Aren't you asking a lot of the Blessed Mother?" the soldier said.

"Yes, but she gives us a lot."

"Listen, Mother Teresa," the soldier said. "If you get your ceasefire tomorrow, I will even go with you to get the children."

"Thank you very much," Mother said with a big smile. "I will meet you here early tomorrow morning."

The next morning there was a ceasefire of sorts. Although everyone else was against the project, Mother Teresa convinced De Salis to send four Red Cross vehicles into West Beirut. She traveled in the first one. When they were crossing the checkpoint, the guard asked, "Are you carrying any weapons?"

"Oh, yes," Mother Teresa said, "my prayer books and my rosary." She held them up.

They found thirty-eight children from ages seven to twenty-one, all helpless. They did not know what was going on, but they knew that they had no food or water and no care and that they all felt weak, uncomfortable and afraid. Mother Teresa shook hands with the older children and patted the younger ones. One by one, she, the Red Cross workers and the hospital workers carried or led the children to the vehicles.

They crossed the Green Line at an Israeli-controlled checkpoint and rushed the children to the convent. Within a short time, the children were all clean, comforted and fed.

People who had lost most of their own possessions brought clothes, food, beds, medical and cleaning supplies. Mother Teresa realized that in wartime most humanitarian efforts are concentrated on casualties. The needs of the blind, the deaf, the insane, the elderly and babies are overlooked.

Two days later Mother Teresa crossed the Green Line again to evacuate another twenty-seven children. A Red Cross worker said, "She saw the problem, fell to her knees, prayed for a few seconds and then rattled off a list of supplies she needed. We didn't expect a saint to be so efficient."

Reporters tried to get political statements from her. Instead she read them Saint Francis' beautiful Peace Prayer, which begins, "Lord, make me an instrument of your peace."

Mother said, "I have never been in a war before, but I have seen famine and death. I don't understand this. Let us not use bombs and guns to overcome the world. Let's use love and compassion."

When some soldiers explained their ideas about defense, Mother said, "Today nations put too much effort and money into defending their borders. If they could only defend defenseless people with food, shelter and clothing, the world would be a happier place."

In wartime when each side dehumanizes its enemy, Mother Teresa was the conscience of both sides with her ability to see the enemy as Jesus in his most distressing disguise.

On May 30 Pope John Paul II said, "Mother Teresa, you look unusually tired. Please go for a medical checkup." On June 2 she was hospitalized in Salvator Mundi hospital after falling out of bed in the convent at San Gregorio in Rome. The doctor said, "Mother Teresa is on the verge of a major heart attack." Mother had to be fed all of her meals. She refused to take prescribed painkillers, saying, "I want to offer up my sufferings to God." She did take the medicine for poor blood circulation to get well to return to her poor.

The world media focused on Mother Teresa the way India's media used to focus on Mohandas Gandhi during his long fasts. People all over the world prayed for Mother. She received get-well cards, letters and telegrams. A priest brought the Eucharist every day for adoration and each day he said a Mass in her room. Mother Teresa's doctors told her, "If you obey instructions and take your medicine, you can live many years. But you must not lift anything, not even babies."

"But you can still hug them, Mother," Ann Blaikie told her.

Right after she left the hospital, Mother Teresa took her sisters to Warsaw.

In less than seven weeks Mother Teresa went to New York to visit her friend Cardinal Cooke, who was dying of cancer. He had given her an empty convent for her new priest Coworker movement called Corpus Christi. It consisted of priests from other orders such as Jesuit, Dominican and parish priests who volunteered to work with the Missionaries of Charity. The Missionaries of Charity brothers were now operating separately, and Mother felt the priest Coworkers would separate also.

When Mother returned for a checkup, her doctors said, "Mother Teresa, the way you live would kill a much younger person with a healthy heart. You must slow down."

"I feel Jesus calling me, and I never say no to him."

Mother told her sisters about a dream she had when she was almost comatose: "I knocked on the gates of heaven and Saint Peter said, 'We're not ready for you, Mother Teresa. You are needed in the slums. There are no slums up here.'"

18

A GREATER VISION

MOTHER TERESA DID NOT SLOW DOWN. IN NOVEMBER 1983, ONLY SIX months after she was put on heart medication, Mother Teresa flew to Hong Kong to see her sisters in the center opened earlier that year. While there, Mother met with Queen Elizabeth II in Delhi to receive one of Britain's greatest honors, the Order of Merit.

In April 1984 she addressed young people in St. Peter's Square in Rome and later at the Coliseum, where Brother Roger of Taize joined her.

For many years Chinese bishops and priests who retained a link with Rome were jailed and even killed. Chinese Catholics had to give their allegiance to the Chinese Patriotic Church in order to worship openly. Pope John Paul II was eager to establish ties with China's Patriotic Church, and Mother Teresa hoped that she and the Missionaries of Charity could help accomplish this.

The communist authorities in China told Mother Teresa that there were no poor there. "I am delighted to hear that you have no poor, but there may be some people who could use our encouragement."

An official said, "We could allow your sisters to do that much."

Mother insisted that a Roman Catholic priest go with her sisters since a Chinese priest would not recognize the pope. The Chinese felt Mother should accept a priest from the Chinese Patriotic Catholic Church.

So instead of going to China, she addressed a worldwide retreat of priests in Rome. Her words were translated into several languages since the priests came from every continent and represented every race. All were inspired by the tiny nun sharing her unconditional love. Mother said simply, "Be holy like Jesus."

After the Rome retreat several priests formed the Missionaries of Charity Fathers. "I don't think I'll start anything more," Mother Teresa said. At seventy-four years old she had just added a new society to her spiritual family.

On October 31, 1984, after the Indian military stormed the Sikhs' sacred temple, Mother's friend Indira Gandhi was assassinated. Mother attended the cremation. Several Sikhs were killed in reprisal, and Mother Teresa and her sisters visited Sikhs who were hiding for fear they'd be killed.

In December 1984, when poisonous gas escaped from a plant in Bhopal, India, Mother and her sisters flew there. Over twenty-five thousand people died and many more were seriously harmed. On Christmas Mother Teresa brought food and medicine to Ethiopia, a country disrupted by war and drought. She even opened a home there. When Mother Teresa asked President Reagan for help, he reached villages cut off by government forces that confiscated the food for themselves.

One million people died of starvation during the Ethiopian famine, but seven million people threatened with death by starvation were saved by these massive efforts.

In January 1985 the Patriotic Catholic Church invited Mother Teresa to China. The Chinese government treated her kindly. Since China had no convents, Mother stayed in a luxury hotel.

She went to a Latin Mass at Immaculate Conception Church. She met Deng Pufang, the prime minister's son who was in a wheelchair since Red guards threw him out a window during the Cultural Revolution and broke his back. Deng Pufang headed

China's Welfare Fund for the Handicapped. "We both want to help our people."

Mother said, "The same loving hand has created you and me. What you do is your love for God in action."

"I am an atheist," Deng said.

He arranged for Mother Teresa to visit a factory for the disabled. Mother examined the work of over two hundred factory workers, many of them blind, and wrote in the visitor's book; "God bless you all. Pray for me."

"We owe everything to the Communist Party," Deng said.

Asked if she had a message from the Vatican to the estranged Chinese Patriotic Catholic Association, she replied, "No, I'm coming from Calcutta."

As before, Mother refused a Chinese Patriotic priest and explained that a Roman Catholic priest had to be available for the sisters.

Mother Teresa was disappointed that she could not open a home in China now, but she assured the government that sisters would come to China any time they were allowed a Roman Catholic priest.

Mother was often criticized for appearing with heads of countries, politicians and famous people and accepting awards. But thanks to her high profile, her "poorest of the poor" were known to the world, loved and cared for.

On August 24, 1985, Mother Teresa spent her seventy-fifth birthday at the motherhouse in Calcutta. One month later the general chapter met at the motherhouse. On October 1 Mother Teresa was elected superior general once more.

On October 26, to celebrate their fortieth anniversary, the United Nations showed "The World of Mother Teresa," and Secretary General Xavier Perez de Cuellar introduced Mother Teresa as "the most powerful woman in the world."

She handed out copies of Saint Francis' Peace Prayer to everyone in the audience, and said, "No color, no religion, no nationality should come between us, for we are all children of the same loving God. We are all afraid of nuclear war and of this terrible new disease. But we are not afraid to kill an innocent unborn child."

Reporters asked, "Mother Teresa, what do you think of the nuclear arms race?"

"I don't know much about that," she said, "but I do know anything that destroys life is evil."

A reporter asked, "What do you think about a just war, Mother?"

She said, "War is killing human beings. How could this ever be just?"

"But your church teaches there can be a just war," the reporter said.

"I could never agree to the taking of a human life," Mother kept shaking her head.

"Catholics have to believe in the teaching about just war," the reporter insisted.

"Then I'm not a good Catholic?" Mother said.

When Mother spoke of a "terrible new disease" she meant AIDS. She heard many babies in New York were born with AIDS, so she asked Mayor Ed Koch about opening a home for children with the disease.

"Mother Teresa, I am happy you want to open a house for AIDS victims," he said. "AIDS is the number-one killer of men in their thirties in New York City. Could you open a home for them, Mother?"

On Christmas Eve 1985 Mother opened "Gift of Love," her home for AIDS patients in Greenwich Village. Four sisters cared for the fifteen men who came there with AIDS.

The first to die was Harvey, a Vietnam War veteran with a history of drug abuse. He said, "Sister, please bring Father to baptize me." The priest baptized him and gave him the last rites.

"Do you want to go to heaven?" a sister asked.

"Oh, yes, but I don't want to leave this house. It is so full of love and peace."

"The love and peace here comes from Jesus, and you will see him face-to-face in heaven," the sisters said.

"Teach me to talk to God."

They taught him the Lord's Prayer and said, "Talk to God the way you would talk to your own father and don't forget to listen to his answers."

A sister brought the Bible, and they read Psalm 32:

Happy are those whose transgression is forgiven,
    whose sin is covered.
Happy are those to whom the LORD imputes no iniquity,
    and in whose spirit there is not deceit.
While I kept silence, my body wasted away
    through my groaning all day long.
For day and night your hand was heavy upon me;
    my strength was dried up as by the heat of summer.
Then I acknowledged my sin to you,
    and I did not hide my iniquity;
I said, "I will confess my transgression to the LORD,"
    and you forgave the guilt of my sin.

When they finished the psalm, Harvey died peacefully as did most of those who died in the loving care of the Missionaries of Charity.

Whenever Pope John Paul II traveled, he followed certain rituals. When he landed in a country, he knelt and kissed the ground. His first stop was a church. However, in February 1986 in Calcutta he went directly to Mother Teresa's home for the dying. He went with Mother Teresa from cot to cot, bending to touch each person, helping to feed the weakest. "Come back again," a Hindu woman said.

The pope entered the little morgue with Mother and blessed the four men who had died that day. When he was leaving, Mother Teresa said, "Thank you, Holy Father, for blessing us with your visit."

"Thank you, Mother Teresa, for reminding everyone that God is in love with each one of us and never stops trying to win our love."

After the pope left, Mother Teresa said, "I have had many happy days, but this is the happiest day of my life."

19

Eight Days and Nights

Even though she was frail and sickly, Mother Teresa continued to seek out the poorest around the world. In August 1988 she went to Nepal to help earthquake victims.

That year, several bishops went to China to seek the reunion of Chinese Catholics. They told Mother that she and her sisters would be welcome there on two conditions: the work must be social, not religious, and the sisters must dress in the Chinese style. Mother agreed to these conditions and hoped to establish a home there. But the Chinese still refused to allow a Roman Catholic priest.

She founded a convent in Khayelitsha, a black township outside of Cape Town, South Africa. Although she was accused of having political goals, she said, "I did not know that apartheid existed. White, black, green, yellow, whatever, you are God's children, created to love and be loved."

In early September 1989 Mother became critically ill. When her vomiting and high fever continued, she was taken to Woodland Nursing Home in Calcutta. She remained in intensive care, watched over by her Italian doctor and an American doctor. Mother Teresa had angina pectoris. Two of her arteries were completely blocked. The world prayed for her. India's president and many other heads of state sent messages. The doctors implanted a pacemaker and Mother recovered enough to continue her mission.

In late 1989 the people of communist East Germany began dismantling the Berlin Wall. Erected in 1961 to discourage refugees from seeking freedom in the West, it symbolized tyranny, the Iron Curtain. When it came down, the world rejoiced. Citizens of Hungary, Romania and other repressed countries rose against their communist leaders, who had controlled them for years.

In spite of ill health, Mother went right away to the countries whose religious needs were most pressing. She opened five houses in the USSR and one in Armenia. She established a children's home in Bucharest for young AIDS victims and two homes in Czechoslovakia.

During Holy Week 1990, before her eightieth birthday, Mother asked Pope John Paul II to let her resign as head of her order. He agreed and a general chapter was convened in Calcutta to elect her successor. Many sisters wanted Mother to stay in office until she died; others felt she should train a successor while continuing as their spiritual adviser.

A few days before the election Sister Agnes, the first councilor of the active branch, and Sister Nirmala, head of the contemplative branch, went to Father Van Exem, who was confined to his sickbed, and asked, "Father, can we reelect Mother?" He replied, "There is nothing in church law to prevent it."

Worldwide, the media frenzy escalated. Who would replace Mother? Mother and her sisters met twelve miles outside of Calcutta. Iron gates prevented the media from entering the compound. Eight days and nights of prayer and silence preceded the election. When the results were announced, Mother was the winner. The media around the world was shocked but her sisters rejoiced. They still had Mother's special magic that opened hearts everywhere. "I had expected to be free," Mother admitted, "but God has his own plans."

Lying in hospital beds, keeping death at bay, Mother held onto her dearest dreams, to open houses in China and in Albania, where her mother and sister were buried.

Albania was the last stronghold of communism in eastern Europe. In the spring of 1990, when Mother asked to open a house there, the communist regime was defensive. They said, "It would break the law to open a home."

"Then I will break the law," Mother said. But the ban on religion was lifted, and citizens could practice their religions without punishment. The new head of Albania, Ramiz Alia, welcomed her. "The world calls you Mother Teresa of Calcutta. But we call you Mother Teresa of Albania." Soon she had four houses in Albania.

No country was too far away, no danger too frightening for Mother and her Missionaries of Charity. In August 1990 Iraq invaded Kuwait. The United Nations demanded a complete withdrawal of all Iraqi forces, but Iraq's leader, Saddam Hussein, would not move. President George H.W. Bush threatened to retaliate if Iraq didn't free Kuwait, from which the United States imported a large amount of oil. Concerned about the threat of war, Mother wrote a joint letter to Bush and Hussein. "I come to you with tears in my eyes and God's love in my heart," she said. "I plead to you for those who will be left orphaned, widowed and alone because their parents, husbands, brothers and children have been killed. I beg you to save them. Please choose the way of peace."

They both ignored Mother and the U.S. and its allies sent over six hundred thousand troops for a massive attack on Iraq. Saddam Hussein's troops were defeated in a mere four days. After the cease-fire, Hussein invited Mother to Baghdad where she found terrible destruction. She opened a home for the elderly, and one for crippled and ill children.

In late 1991 Mother Teresa went to Tijuana, Mexico, the world's fastest-growing border town. "I have never seen worse poverty," she remarked. After visiting the Missionaries of Charity soup kitchen, the home for the elderly and the convent, she went to the seminary for the ordination Mass of a Missionaries of Charity brother.

Mother celebrated the Feast of Our Lady of Guadalupe in Tijuana on December 12. Shortly after that, she had a serious heart attack and was transferred to Scripps Hospital in La Jolla, California. She was cared for by the country's top specialists, including Dr. Anita Figueredo.

Again the world prayed for Mother's survival. On Super Bowl Sunday Bishop Robert Brom of San Diego visited Mother Teresa at the Hospital in La Jolla and asked how she was feeling. "I feel like I am the football being kicked here and there. God is moving me around until I get in the place where he wants me." During the bishop's visit, Pope John Paul II called. Mother was near death at the time, so the bishop took the call. He handed the phone to Mother Teresa. Her arm shook as she held it. She listened a minute, then put the receiver on her bed and said, "He said he loves me." She picked up the phone and said, "Holy Father, I love you too. And I love the whole world." No one in the room had dry eyes.

In early 1992 en route to Calcutta Mother Teresa became ill again in Rome and was admitted to the hospital. Someone asked, "Mother, are you afraid of death?" She said, "Oh, no! I see it every day. Death is the shortest way to God. It's the way home."

Mother had planned to meet Diana, Princess of Wales, in Calcutta. When Diana arrived she learned Mother was ill in Rome. Nonetheless, she went to Nirmal Hriday, the home for the dying. She touched the bodies of the suffering, showing them love and compassion.

Mother spent her eighty-third birthday in the Institute of Medical Science Hospital in New Delhi. She had fever and vomiting, lung congestion and heart problems. But the next day she boarded a plane for Calcutta.

By September 17 Mother Teresa was once more fighting for her life. Surgeons attempted to clear a blocked heart vessel. While she was in intensive care, Father Celeste Van Exem, her spiritual director, wrote her a letter saying that he was offering his life that she might live and open a house in China. He died shortly after that at St. Xavier's College in Calcutta.

Mother returned to China in 1993 and again in March of 1994. Both times she met with Deng Pufang hoping to reach an agreement. She never gave up trying to open a home in China. "It looks like China needs more prayers," she said.

In April 1996 Mother fell and broke her collarbone. In June she broke her foot but kept traveling in a wheelchair. Somehow she managed to open her 565th house in Wales. By the end of August she was again in intensive care at Woodland's Nursing Home in Calcutta and could only breathe with a respirator.

On the eve of her eighty-sixth birthday, surprising her doctors, Mother could breathe without a respirator, and by September 6 she felt well enough to be released. But by September 25 she was back in the hospital. On December 19, 1996, Mother returned to the motherhouse, where she was confined to bed with severe back pain.

In January 1997 Mother Teresa resigned as Superior General due to poor health.

Once more the Missionaries of Charity spent eight days and nights in silent prayer before the election of Mother's successor. On March 13, 1997, they chose Sister Nirmala, former head of the contemplative sisters. At Pope John Paul II's suggestion, Mother remained spiritual head and helped the newly-elected superior general.

Most people expected Mother's replacement to come from the active branch, but Mother Teresa had always said, "We can't do physical works of mercy unless we spend time in meditation, listening to the Lord."

On June 5, 1997, Mother received the Congressional Medal of Honor in Washington, D.C., for "outstanding and enduring contributions to humanity." When she was at her convent in the South Bronx, Princess Diana visited her for the last time. When a Coworker announced her arrival, Mother said, "I'm busy right now." She never raised her head but continued to wash the human skeleton lying on the thin mattress. "Show the princess how she can be helpful." Princess Diana made her way down the rows of suffering bodies. Her cheerful smile comforted the dying; words of encouragement gave hope to the lonely and her hands administered to the sick. Her love and compassion were the qualities that endeared her to Mother Teresa.

Little did the world know that both would be gone before the summer was over.

20

SAFELY HOME

ON THE MORNING OF SEPTEMBER 3, 1997, MOTHER ASKED HER OLD friend, Michael Gomes (who still lived at 14 Creek Lane) to take her to St. John's Church Cemetery where she expected to be buried one day. She prayed at a Missionary of Charity sister's grave. The next day she and Michael returned.

The rains were coming down the night of September 5. Mother Teresa was planning to attend a memorial service at St. Paul's Cathedral in Calcutta for Princess Diana, who had been killed in an automobile accident in Paris only a few days earlier.

That evening Mother Teresa dictated her final letter to the Missionaries of Charity and Coworkers.

At 9:00 PM Mother had a sharp pain in her chest, fell on her mat and passed out. Sister Nirmala called the doctor. He was there when Mother came to and said, "I can't breathe." Then she said, "Jesus, I love you." In moments she was gone. All the sisters rushed to her room, hugged her and cried. By midnight people surrounded the convent, mourning Calcutta's own saint.

Mother's body was embalmed, wrapped in an Indian flag, taken to St. Thomas Church in a Missionaries of Charity ambulance and put on view. Her feet were bare.

India gave Mother a state funeral similar to Gandhi's, using the same gun carriage that had carried Gandhi's body. Sister Nirmala reserved half of the fifteen thousand available seats at the funeral for lepers, orphans and the poor. The rains continued as fifty thousand people came each day to say good-bye.

Pope John Paul II celebrated a Mass for her at Castel Gandolfo, his summer residence. Advancing in age and in poor health, he sent Cardinal Sadano with his message: "She has left her mark on the history of this century. She was a glowing example of how the love of God can be transformed to the love of one's neighbor. Dear Mother Teresa, rest in peace. Dear Mother Teresa, pray for all."

Mother Teresa and Princess Diana were two of the most famous women of the twentieth century. They had much love and respect for each other. That they should die the same week stunned the world. The ongoing news coverage of Diana's death, however, overshadowed that of Mother Teresa's. It was as though Princess Diana's spirit was saying to Mother Teresa's, "I have died first, still young, with some mystery surrounding my death, and you, who have given so much, can slip into heaven unnoticed."

Mother Teresa's final resting place is a simple room in the Calcutta motherhouse where she lived and worked. The universe echoes her words of comfort: "They are with the Father. They're safely home."

Part Two

WHAT
MOTHER
TERESA
TAUGHT
ME

"We are not social workers.
We are contemplatives in the world
touching the body of Christ
twenty-four hours."
–Mother Teresa,
on receiving the Nobel prize

21

A Ticket to Saint Peter

When Mother Teresa won the Nobel Peace Prize in 1979, I was substitute teaching the geography and history of India at St. Joseph's High School in Hawaii. Many students borrowed the books about Mother Teresa I brought to class. They were composing an encyclopedia of India, with each student writing on several topics. Because most students wanted to write about Mother, I decided to write a book about her, keeping young adults in mind. I researched, writing to every name I came across with a connection with Mother Teresa. Almost every one answered and many corresponded with me for years.

When I tried to reach her Coworkers in Hawaii, I was given a name and address on the Big Island where I lived and was asked to organize a group. Later I learned if you ask the Coworkers for anything worthwhile that doesn't yet exist, they expect you to create it.

At ten o'clock one morning my sister Susie called to say our brother John's doctors had given him seventy-two hours to live. I did not know he was ill. John was my twelve-year-old son Raphael's godfather. I phoned Raphael's teachers, and told them there was a death in the family. Three hours later, leaving the house, I told Raphael, "You might want to bring a few of your treasures just in case we don't return."

"I'd like to take my guitar," he said, but soon decided it would slow us down. He left it.

I grabbed a handmade crucifix I had inherited from my godmother Kathleen, whom we called "Aunt Sis." On one side was Jesus and on the other Mary. I knew Mother Teresa would appreciate the fact that an image of the Blessed Mother was on the cross. Mother called Mary "the cause of our joy" and reminded us that without Mary we would not have Jesus.

By one o'clock Raphael and I were on a plane to Ohio. I calmed myself by reading Mother's words about beautiful deaths, descriptions of people who died in her homes with "a ticket to Saint Peter." I read of the man who said, "I am going home to God," then closed his eyes and went home. Mother said over twenty-two thousand people died making an act of love for God. Her faith comforted me on that long flight.

We arrived in time to tell John good-bye. My mother, father and nine brothers and sisters were at the hospital along with John's wife, Patti, and his two sons, Jon-Jon and Louie. John's six-month-old daughter Lauren was across town in the children's hospital with a huge tumor in her chest. Patti said, "I have been going from one hospital to the next, praying both John and Lauren will live but if one or both of them die that I can share their last moments."

When Raphael and I entered John's room, he said, "My godson! It's so wonderful to see you." John's skin was gray and he was so weak he had a hard time hugging us. "I need my rosaries," he said. Patti couldn't find them in her purse.

Mother Teresa loved the rosary and encouraged everyone to say it often, so I always carried my rosaries with me. But I had changed purses and left them at home. I handed John Aunt Sis's crucifix and he held it tight. A nurse burst into the room shouting, "Mrs. Patterson, the children's hospital called. Your baby is dying! They want you immediately."

Patti had not wanted John to know the baby was ill. Poor John tried to get out of bed. "I'm going with you," he said. "I have to see my precious Lauren." The nurse told John he must stay in bed but he fought to get up. She called for help and a huge man tied my dying brother to his bed. He sobbed for his little girl. John never let go of Aunt Sis's crucifix, and died clinging to it.

Patti asked if she could keep the crucifix since it was the last item John held. I told her she could bury him with it or keep it herself.

Little Lauren was near death for a few weeks but slowly healed and is now a lovely young woman who recently gave birth to her first child, Ryan Jon Patrick.

It was the first death in our immediate family and brought the remaining brothers and sisters closer together. Instead of returning to Hawaii, Raphael and I remained with our family in Ohio.

22

FINDING CALCUTTA IN MY HOMETOWN

"YOU CAN FIND CALCUTTA ALL OVER THE WORLD IF YOU HAVE EYES TO see," Mother said. "Begin in your own home, your own neighborhood." I grew up in Waverly, Ohio, a little village at the foothills of the Appalachian Mountains. But it wasn't until I returned to Ohio and began working with the poor that I discovered what poverty existed a few miles from my home.

Helen Bacon, the Ohio link for Mother Teresa's Coworkers, gave me permission to start a group of young Coworkers, which consisted of Raphael, his friends and schoolmates. We worked on various projects: spiritual work to praise the Lord and to grow closer to him, social programs to learn to love one another and service projects to show our love for God and neighbor. They planned their own prayer services and a Christmas liturgy, and served as eucharistic ministers, lecturers, ushers and acolytes.

At Christmas they had a "giving tree" where they collected gifts for poor families. On the back of ornaments they wrote the items needed by the family–toy for a two-year-old, mittens for six-year-old, size twelve dress for a woman. They put the tree in the back of the church, and after Mass, parishioners took ornaments, bought and wrapped the gifts and returned them under the tree with the ornament for identification.

The young people delivered the gifts. We went into the hollows of the Appalachian Mountains that surrounded our town. I had never seen such poverty. Large families lived in one-room shacks, often with no heat, though the weather was below zero. Many people had no running water and no electricity. Some children had no shoes and only a few blankets. The mountain people were proud and would never ask for help, but they smiled and invited us inside where we sang Christmas carols and they opened their presents.

On Christmas Eve one poor, elderly woman's house burned down. What upset her most was losing her precious cat in the fire. The Coworkers went from store to store telling the woman's story and replacing her lost items. My sister Susie insisted that we wrap every item since it was Christmas and we wanted to cheer up the woman.

I went to Cleveland to meet Ann Blaikie, Mother Teresa's first Coworker. Ann had written me some beautiful letters about the beginnings of the Coworkers. I will never forget her words: "I was coordinating an international Coworkers' conference in Rome where Mother Teresa and the Holy Father were speaking. Just as I was leaving my house, my neighbor arrived. 'My sister just died,' she said, 'and I'm all alone.' I called Rome to say I couldn't make the conference and spent the weekend consoling my neighbor. I knew that was what Mother Teresa would want. She always says our caring must begin at home."

While I was in Waverly, my parish, St. Mary, Queen of the Missions, asked me to coordinate its outreach center serving the poor. Being a Coworker, I used everything I had learned from Mother Teresa to help me work with St. Mary's center. Every Friday the volunteers gathered in the parish hall to prepare clothing and other items to give to the poor. Mother Teresa said "Everything should begin with prayer." We began each session with a short prayer.

The church asked us to make up a constitution. My suggestions came from what I'd learned from Mother. We began with some Scriptures Mother Teresa often quoted:

"Just as you did it to one of the least of these who are members of my family, you did it to me" (Matthew 25:40).

"Those who say 'I love God', and hate their brothers or sisters, are liars; for those who do not love a brother or sister whom they have seen, cannot love God whom they have not seen" (1 John 4:20).

"[L]ove the Lord your God with all your heart, and with all your soul, and with all your mind, and with all your strength.... [L]ove your neighbor as yourself" (Mark 12:30-31).

In the parable of the Good Samaritan, Jesus tells us that our neighbor is anyone who needs our help.

St. Mary's center was inspired by Mother Teresa's words: "If sometimes our poor people have died of starvation, it is not because God didn't care for them, but because you and I didn't give, were not instruments of love in God's hands, to give them that bread, to give them that clothing, because we did not recognize Christ in distressing disguise in the hungry man, in the lonely man, in the homeless child seeking shelter."

Like Mother Teresa's Coworkers, St. Mary's center was an ecumenical organization of men, women and children of various faiths who sought to love God in their neighbors through whole hearted free service to the poor. Following Mother Teresa's example, we made our work a prayer by doing it in God's presence, with him and to him. We did "small things with great love to create something beautiful for God."

Like Mother, we preached without preaching, by our example, by our actions. St. Mary's center was a source of evangelization through our sharing the experience of Jesus with others, reaching out to those in need, making them feel welcome, exchanging ideas, sharing concerns, working together for solutions to social problems.

There was never any guarantee that we could fulfill a material need–although we did our best–and many people believed that was why they came. Once they were here, they often forgot for a while their desperate needs as we shared a moment of love. Even without speaking his name (although it was often spoken), we felt Jesus' presence. I remembered how Mother Teresa always led us to the chapel to greet the master of the house.

A woman who lost her home, her sister, everything she owned in a fire came to share her grief. As we replaced some of her worldly goods, she showed us a photo of her beloved sister and told us how her family had lived in that house for generations. She left having found a new family, and promised to return.

A family with no transportation walked five miles to the center and carefully chose clothes to take home because even a few clothes weighed heavy on the long walk. This same family carried clothing to us whenever they received new clothes that were too small for their children.

A woman found an elegant shoe that fit her perfectly, but couldn't find the mate so she brought it back each Friday until that Cinderella day when the second shoe magically appeared.

A volunteer named Loretta gathered scraps of lace and bits of bright material to make dolls and toy animals for the children at our Christmas party.

Just when a mother was telling us her ten-month-old baby slept on a chair at home, a parishioner brought a crib. I recognized the daily little miracles Mother Teresa talked about.

One Friday a woman grabbed all of the baby clothes. A few minutes later a young, very pregnant woman said, "I don't have anything to put on my baby, and she is due any day now." The first woman reached into her bag and handed all the baby clothes to the pregnant woman. "You keep some," the pregnant woman replied. "That's OK," the first said. "My daughter is not due for two months. I'll come back next Friday and find something for her."

An old man said, "I never did like Catholics, but I got to admit you all are good to poor people. I wish the people at my church cared this much about me."

Volunteer Peggy was in the back of the truck packing down an enormous load of clothing when she fell between the clothing stacks and we had to pull her out feet first.

Volunteer Doris wanted a tarp for the truck because rain was threatening and we had sixty miles to go. She opened the phone book and dialed the first number that mentioned tarps. She explained we had no money, and they agreed to make a donation. They were just around the corner. The man made himself a receipt for the tarp for tax purposes. He misunderstood our name and thought we identified ourselves as "St. Mary's Sinner." Doris signed the invoice and became known as St. Mary's Sinner.

One Friday we distributed clothing in an unheated store with icicles hanging from the window. Another time we distributed clothing from the cars because it was warmer there.

After a long illness volunteer Annie Bolen called to say, "I'll be with you girls Friday." She went home to her Lord on Thursday. We talked about closing the center, but Doris reminded us that Annie promised to be there and we couldn't let her down so we said an extra prayer for St. Mary's saint.

We took a woman to visit her two children whom she mistakenly signed away thinking she was signing papers so that her sister-in-law could get medical care for them if necessary.

Doris felt sad leaving her sister Nellie alone in the hospital when, like an angel, our own nurse Jeanie, who "just happened to be on duty," promised to watch over Nellie all night. As Mother Teresa tells us, God loves to show his tender mercy.

Volunteer Chris washed and sewed torn doll clothes, scrubbed old toys, wrapped them in bright paper and stored them in her house until the Christmas party.

When we gave away brand new school shoes, a family with eight children found only seven pairs. We searched and prayed until suddenly the eighth pair appeared, an exact fit, one of God's little miracles, minor to all those around, major to the little boy who had no shoes.

The volunteers took flowers and a stuffed rabbit to a little girl having a serious operation. She entertained and enlightened us with songs about Jesus and the beautiful white gown she'll wear when she gets to heaven.

One Friday Bishop James Griffin of Columbus helped us unload a truckful of clothing in the rain.

All the volunteers cried at Big Brenda's funeral. Brenda was so heavy she had a hard time getting inside the door. Her legs were purple and swollen, but she was filled with the Holy Spirit and always smiled as she looked for something large enough to wear. She was only in her thirties, and her spirit was even younger. She went home to her Lord suddenly. Her husband came and looked through clothes half-heartedly. He enjoyed sharing the Good News, knowing that Jesus *is* with us. And Brenda might drop by to smile on us.

Once we drove miles into the country, only to find a load of rotten and decayed items that we had to pay to throw in the city dump.

One time, when we returned to the truck after we bought toys for the Christmas party, all our sheets, pillowcases and blankets were gone. "What will we do for our burnouts?"

"Someone in Newark must have a bigger emergency," Laura said. We laughed, which was our official response when we didn't know what to say.

A volunteer burst out crying at the Christmas party for which we had spent four hours wrapping presents for the poor. Her husband had recently lost his job, and they could not buy a single present for their own kids. So we gave her presents for each of them.

At times all we had to offer was a smile or a tear, but sometimes our poor needed attention more than a coat or a pair of shoes. They needed to know we love them and God loves them.

An old lady, all bent over, wearing a ragged sweater in the middle of winter, came upon the coat of her dreams, tried it on, looked at herself in the mirror and the years melted away as she stood tall. When volunteers offered her a nice dress, she smiled and said, "No, thank you. I have everything I need."

At the Holy Family soup kitchen in Columbus, when she noticed a prostitute's worn-out shoes, Laura gave the woman her own and returned home barefooted.

Danny was a mentally disabled young man who loved to help but always complained about how many heavy bags he carried. Doris told him, "Just remember, Danny, when you get to heaven, I'll already be there and I'll say, 'Here's Danny, Lord. He used to carry all those bags of clothing for poor people on earth.' " Danny laughed. "And I can hear Our Lord saying, 'Come on in, Danny. I have some bags of clothing for you to carry.'"

23

WORKING WITH TEENAGE GANGS
IN NEW YORK

I LEFT OHIO FOR NEW YORK CITY TO WRITE A BOOK ABOUT AKITA DOGS.
I volunteered as a Vista worker, the domestic version of the Peace
Corps, and worked with the Sisters of St. Joseph caring for
teenagers who had been in trouble with the law.

My first evening at the center I heard some young Puerto
Ricans planning a rumble. They were confident I didn't understand
Spanish, so they went into detail about time and place. When they
finished, I spoke to them in Spanish. There was no gang fight that
night.

I was surprised to learn that many of the young people carried
guns or knives. If we saw a weapon, we were to keep it until the
young man or woman left, then we returned it to them. "Why don't
we just keep the weapons?" I asked. One of the sisters answered, "If
we did, none of them would return. If they didn't come here they
would be out fighting." Although I felt uncomfortable with
weapons, I reminded myself that Mother Teresa would call each of
the youngsters Jesus in his most distressing disguise. How could I
be afraid of Jesus?

On my second evening at the center, I discovered a young man
using a hammer to pull nails out of benches. I said, "I'm sorry but
you have to give me that hammer until you are ready to leave."

He said, "This hammer is my protection. I need it."

"Then you have to leave the center. I will walk you to the door."

He noticed my necklace, a gold heart on a chain. "If you let me hold your chain," he said, "I will give you my hammer."

"My baby's father gave me that heart. It is precious to me," I said.

"It can't mean more to you than the hammer does to me," he insisted. "It is my protection." Impulsively, I handed him the chain and took the hammer. All evening I wondered if I had made a mistake, but when it was time to go home, the young man handed me my gold chain and I returned his hammer.

Later I learned that this young man–I will call him José–led one of the largest gangs in Brooklyn. Though he never spoke kindly to me, he may have saved my life several times. Just as Mother Teresa's sisters live in the community they serve, Vista volunteers live in the area they serve. So Raphael and I lived in a rough Brooklyn neighborhood. There were frequent gang fights, and sometimes participants or passersby got killed. I worked until 9:00 PM and, although I had only a few blocks to walk, I never felt safe until I was home.

One evening as we were leaving, José complained about something that had happened that day. He followed me all the way home shouting that I had messed him up. The next morning I learned there had been a shooting near my home. And almost every time there was a rumble, one of José's friends would walk home behind me telling me what a terrible person I was, but staying with me until I was safely inside.

24

Meeting Mother Teresa
the First Time

One day I received a postcard from Hawaii: "You have a good friend in Brooklyn. My girlfriend, Sister Frances [I have changed her name here], and I were engaged when she fell in love with Jesus. She became one of Mother Teresa's nuns. Find her, tell her you and Raphael are our adopted family and she will welcome you."

Right away I wrote to Sister Frances: "Sister Frances, Missionary of Charity Working with Mother Teresa in Brooklyn." I put the envelope in the mail and forgot about it. Two months later I received a phone call. "Hello, this is Sister Frances. I got your letter even though I no longer live in New York. I am here right now and would like you to come this weekend when I make my vows."

I told her, "I am working with some Catholic nuns caring for troubled teens, and I don't know if I can get away."

"Tell the sisters you are going to meet Mother Teresa," she said. "They will make arrangements for you to come." So I was going to meet Mother Teresa. Miracle of miracles.

That was in June 1982. On the morning of the ceremony Raphael and I took the train uptown to the Bronx. When we left the subway, the scene looked like a war zone. One building after another had been demolished. St. Rita's church was large, and a huge crowd had gathered to catch a glimpse of Mother Teresa. We attended a Mass where eight sisters took their vows.

When Mother Teresa walked up to the altar, I was astonished to see how short she was, yet her energy was so powerful she might have been eight feet tall. Her smile and her loving eyes blessed each of us. She told anecdotes about how beautiful the poor are. "I took rice to a large Muslim family. Before they took a bite, the mother carefully divided the food and took half to her Hindu neighbors. 'They are hungry too, Mother,' she said."

I was to hear her tell that story many times and it always sounded fresh and touching. It meant so much to Mother Teresa. She was comfortable with English but had a strong Indian accent. Her voice was soft, yet she mesmerized her audience. I felt she was confiding in me alone and everyone I talked with felt the same. Mother always spoke of Jesus. She saw him in the Blessed Sacrament, the poor, the dying–everyone–and her all consuming love touched us deeply.

After Mass everyone lined up to shake Mother's hand. "God bless you," she told each of us. There was a reception for the new sisters and their families. Raphael and I were Sister Frances's family. When I told Sister Frances I was writing a book about Mother Teresa for young adults, she rushed me over to Mother. Mother reached out her hand, shook mine, smiled and said, "God bless you." I said I was working with young Puerto Rican gang members. "They read biographies of musicians, famous athletes, movie stars or politicians and many of those people had lived sad tragic lives. I want to write books about people who lived joyful, meaningful lives. That's why I want to write about you, Mother Teresa."

"Write about the work," she said.

I told her that when I was young, my favorite books were about famous people when they were children. Each became my playmate because they remained a child until the last chapter. At the end of the book I was proud of my friends' accomplishments when they grew up. I asked, "Mother, would you tell me a little about your childhood?"

"Write about the work," Mother said again with a big smile. Our conversation was interrupted many times. Everyone was eager to speak with Mother Teresa. She smiled at everyone.

Sister Frances wanted me to meet the other nuns. She told them about my book. Each sister brought me back to Mother Teresa, and once more Mother squeezed my hand, smiled and we resumed our conversation. I continued my questions, and each time, Mother replied, "Write about the work."

"Mother, what was your favorite color when you were a child?" She reached for my hand. "Don't write about me."

"But Mother, young people need to read about people who have found their paths," I protested. Finally Mother said, "We'll see."

My research led me to Michael Gomes, the man in whose upper room Mother Teresa first began her Missionaries of Charity. I was overjoyed when I received a letter from him, with a return address of 14 Creek Lane, Calcutta, the locale now famous in Mother's history.

From the beginning Michael was excited about my book. He answered every letter giving me wonderful information and encouragement. He gladly answered all my questions and offered many beautiful stories about the happy days when Mother Teresa and her first Missionaries of Charity sisters lived in his house. Whenever he or anyone in his family was ill, he would ask me to pray for them, and he prayed for my family and the success of the book. We soon became close friends.

When Michael and his wife Agnes came to the United States to visit their daughter Mabel and her son Patrick, he phoned me hoping we could get together. But he was in Alabama, and I was in California, and neither of us was able to make the trip. Nevertheless, we remained friends and faithful pen pals.

Michael and Agnes stayed close to Mother Teresa, and in each letter Michael would tell me about the last time he had seen her. After Mother died, Michael wrote me that Mother Teresa had asked him to take her to the Catholic cemetery in Calcutta the day before she died so she could pray for her nuns buried there.

Michael continued to write to me until the month he died. His letters were always informative, inspiring and supportive.

Mabel Gomes, the child who went to the slums with Mother Teresa, wrote me her father had died. Agnes sent me a prayer card from Michael's funeral. I wrote Agnes a sympathy card and she answered with a long letter telling me how much I had meant to her husband. She and I became pen pals, writing letters back and forth the way Michael and I had done.

Another lifetime friend of mine is Jacqueline de Decker. My first letter to Jacqueline was in French, but she insisted I write her in English because I spelled God *Dieux* in French, which means more than one god. "I hope you aren't writing your book in French," she begged. Jacqueline answered all my letters and gave me wonderful information. I sent her pictures of Raphael and me, and she began signing her letters "Aunt Jacqueline."

Not long after we met Mother Teresa, our friends Fred and Taia Chard invited Raphael and me to return to Hawaii and live with them. We flew to California and stopped in San Rafael. Raphael and I went to Mass at the old mission and visited the bookshop. A young girl asked me, "Have you seen any books about Saint Clare?" I pointed to an entire shelf.

"Have you seen any books about Mother Teresa?" I asked. "Yes, there, against the wall," she said. "When Mother Teresa opened a house in San Francisco, I went to the press conference because I write for my school paper. I got some papers about Mother Teresa's childhood."

I asked if I could see them. "When my priest finishes reading them," she told me.

I gave her my Hawaiian address. Two months later, settled in Hawaii, I received a package from Karen Marie Kitterman in San Rafael with information about Mother's childhood that I had been unable to find elsewhere. I was convinced this was a sign that God wanted me to write about Mother's childhood.

Mother Teresa said we must never let our work with the poor interfere with our family. I was determined to spend time with my son, Raphael, to enjoy his presence before he was grown and on his own, but each time he came to me eager to talk or share some insight, I found myself in the middle of a sentence I'd struggled to write or cooking something that demanded my undivided attention. I realized I was only half listening, offering half of myself. By watching Mother Teresa, who was one of the busiest people in the world, I learned to spend precious time with my son.

Mother encouraged family prayer. Raphael and I began saying grace aloud together and sharing nightly prayers, in which we prayed from the heart about whatever mattered most to us at the moment.

By chance I met a nun who had recently heard Mother Teresa speak on natural birth control in Mexico. Although Mother Teresa did not believe in artificial birth control, she believed that natural family planning should be taught to any married woman who was interested. The sister told me, "Mother Teresa and her sisters are teaching natural family planning to the poor in Calcutta."

A few months later I went to New York where I worked in the soup kitchen run by Mother's sisters. It was located in the same building in the South Bronx on 145th street where I first met Mother.

I was staying with friends on the Lower East Side. To arrive at 6:00 AM for Mass, I had to leave home at 4:30 AM. It was still dark and

I was alone on the New York subway. I thought about how the sisters usually traveled by two's and wished I had a partner. I looked at my watch when I came out of the subway. It was 5:30 AM. Strange shadows and crumbling ruins looked menacing as I walked down the deserted street. From behind a hand touched my arm. I was frightened. A man asked, "Are you lost, lady?" I was relieved when I looked into the kind face of a small, elderly, dark man. I said, "I'm looking for Mother Teresa's Missionaries of Charity." He told me his name was Angel Rafael Rodriguez, and he was delivering newspapers. He said proudly, "I know Mother Teresa's sisters well. I will take you there when I finish my route."

Angel Rodriguez and I finished his rounds. He had a smile and a word for everyone. He walked me to the convent and waited until the sisters answered the door. "Hello, Angel," the young sister said.

"I can't stay this morning, sister, but I brought you a young lady."

"That was kind of you, Angel."

I was glad to take part in the work that happened where I first met Mother Teresa. The sister led me into the chapel. A crucifix hung over the altar with the words, "I Thirst." A few wooden chairs were in the back for visitors who could not kneel or sit on the floor. I asked God to keep me from spoiling the work and to let me be an instrument of his peace, love and healing. Then the sister led me to a large room full of used clothing. "Could you help us sort these so they are ready for our poor people who need them? God bless you," she said and left me alone in the musty room. I looked around, realizing that I didn't know what she wanted me to do. How was I to prepare the clothing?

"Lord, I asked you not to let me spoil the work," I prayed. "Please tell me what to do."

I decided to sort the clothing, putting all the men's clothes together, the women's clothes in their place and the children's in another. Then I separated the clothing by seasons. Usually whenever I had been doing work of this kind, I had lots of Coworkers to help me know what to do. It was a good chance to pray while doing the work. I felt especially close to God there and I prayed that Mother Teresa would give me written permission to write the book so her people would help me. I remembered to ask, "If it is your will, God."

After the clothing project I was invited to cut up vegetables in the soup kitchen. A bell rang and everyone stopped working to pray. At first it seemed strange to see everyone stopping their work in the middle of an action. We managed to get the food ready, and quite a crowd gathered for the meal. The majority were single men but there were some women alone and some with a child or two.

Before I left the convent, I gave the sisters a copy of the first three chapters of my book.

I returned home to the Big Island of Hawaii where I continued to write. One month later I received a letter saying: "Mother Teresa has given you permission to write and publish a book about her work."

25

MRS. RODRIQUEZ

IN 1990 I RENTED A ROOM IN ENCINITAS, CALIFORNIA, FROM MRS. Rodriquez, an elderly Mexican woman who was a Coworker of Mother Teresa. She spoke only Spanish and insisted that I do the same in her house, even with her grown children who were all bilingual. Of my Spanish she said, "I have never heard anyone speaking so much Spanish so poorly." I remember the day there was a fire on the stove, and I screamed, "Fuego! Fuego!" Before she went into the kitchen to see about the fire, she had to correct my pronunciation of *fuego*.

Her home was only a few blocks from St. John's Church, and we walked to Mass together every day. At two o'clock one morning, I was awakened by four gunshots. I tried to pretend I hadn't heard them, but Mrs. Rodriquez was shouting for me.

Three young men from Guatemala were living in a trailer in our backyard. I didn't want to get involved, but I remembered how Mother Teresa said we should be a Good Samaritan and see anyone in need as our neighbor. Saying a quick prayer, I dashed into the yard in my robe and bare feet. Alfonso, one of the young men, was lying on the grass covered with blood. His friend was bending over him. I thought Alfonso must be dead from having lost so much blood. I shouted the Lord's Prayer in Spanish. Alfonso's young friend and Mrs. Rodriquez joined me.

The medics and the police arrived almost simultaneously. Neither had any Spanish-speaking members, and since I was the only bilingual person I translated for the medics. "Please tell him to lie still. He will die unless we get him to the hospital for a transfusion." After the medics lifted Alfonso into the helicopter, the police asked me to translate as they questioned his roommate. Alfonso had been shot by a good friend who was drunk and found a gun in his car.

Mother Teresa was right when she said the first thing to do in any emergency was to pray. Alfonso had four blood transfusions and the doctors said they had never seen anyone lose so much blood and live. After a week he was released from intensive care. Most of our Coworkers visited him and we all prayed for him. Then his friend told us he was depressed because the doctors had amputated his leg above the knee. The Coworkers went to the hospital. "Alfonso is being operated on," the nurse said. We asked if we could wait in his room. She said, "Only his family can see him after the surgery."

"He lives with us," I said. "His family is in Guatemala. We are the only family he has here." They let us wait, and we said a rosary as we knew Mother Teresa would want us to do. When Alfonso came into the room, he was in pain but he was delighted to find us. Mrs. Rodriquez asked Alfonso if his family in Guatemala knew what had happened. "No," he said, "since I have no money to send I told them I was sick, but I didn't say anything about the shooting or losing my leg. I'll tell them when I visit."

The man for whom he had worked three years invited him to live with him and his wife until he could live on his own. Alfonso learned to walk on crutches, and soon he was getting fitted for a new leg. His boss lent him the money saying he could pay it back once he returned to work. When he came to show Mrs. Rodriquez and me his new leg, he was riding a bike. "It looks real," he said proudly.

The next day he went to Tijuana with us Coworkers. The Missionaries had arranged for an artificial leg to be fitted for a young Mexican man who lost his in an accident. Alfonso hoped to inspire the man by showing him how well his artificial leg worked. In Mexico volunteers kept giving Alfonso heavy bundles because he looked so strong and healthy. No one knew he had lost his leg and was just learning to wear a new one except for the Mexican man who had lost his leg. I knew Alfonso must have been in great pain but he was happy, following Mother Teresa's advice, "Love until it hurts."

When we brought Alfonso home, he said, "I want to invite all of you to my baptism and First Communion. I was just waiting until I had my new leg."

One day Mrs. Rodriquez asked me, "Would you accompany me to my village for our biggest fiesta? We can make a private pilgrimage to Uruapan where I was born. I am getting old now and I want to go home for the fiesta before I die."

"What fiesta?" I asked. She said the words in Spanish, but I didn't recognize them, so she explained, "It's forty days before *Easter.*"

"Oh, Carnival," I said.

"No. Carnival is when you make friends with your shadow."

"What do you mean?" I asked.

Mrs. Rodriquez turned down the fire under the beans she was cooking. "You are a Catholic. Surely you know the meaning of Carnival." I remembered Carnival in Rio, the fantastic costumes, the parties, the dancing, the music, the parades, but I couldn't figure out what Mrs. Rodriquez was getting at. "I thought Carnival was a time to get your sins out of your system so you could be good and grow spiritually during Lent."

"That's one way of looking at it," Mrs. Rodriquez said. "In our pueblo Carnival is when we take a good look at ourselves and bring the selves we keep hidden into the open where they can't do so much harm."

"We dress up to encourage our shadows to make friends so we won't be afraid or ashamed of them anymore. If you always wear conservative clothes, then for Carnival you might be a clown. If you pride yourself on your modesty you might dress like a lady of the night."

"Mrs. Rodriquez!" I said. She was an elderly proper Mexican lady who never missed daily Mass and always wore a shawl no matter what the weather. She corrected my manners whenever I forgot to address anyone older as Señor or Señora.

"I'm serious," Mrs. Rodriquez continued. "Carnival is an important step in making a good Lent. It's examining your conscience before the sacrament of confession or reconciliation. But it is the right way to begin Lent. We have to talk about confession one day. Do you realize that our Holy Mother church gives us everything we need to be holy and healthy in mind, body and spirit? There are people I know paying fifty dollars an hour to a psychiatrist when they could get more help for free from a regular confession after a good examination of conscience."

She stirred the beans. "But I was explaining how Carnival is a time of growing closer to God. My people believe as long as we keep our shadows hidden inside, we allow ourselves to see them only in others, often in family, friends, neighbors and we criticize them. We need to forgive our own sins after we turn them over to God in confession and he's done his part."

She grabbed a broom and began sweeping the floor. I had to jump to get out of her way. "So Carnival is when we let our inner children and the strange things living in our dark places come out and introduce themselves." She continued sweeping, and I looked for a spot where I would be out of her way but still able to hear all her words of wisdom.

"But Carnival is not my problem," she said, putting the broom in the corner and picking up the mop. "After more than six hundred

Carnivals, I have met and come to acknowledge most, if not all, the shadow family living in me. When I find myself making fun of a friend or neighbor, it doesn't take me long to see what part of myself I am dealing with. And although I may not shut up right away, at least I no longer fool myself about what's really going on. I know it's my own self, one of my shadows I am really talking about."

Her cat came strutting into the kitchen and let out a meow. Mrs. Rodriquez said, "I told you not to come into the kitchen when I am cleaning." She pushed the cat away with her mop.

"I wanted to tell you why I have to be home for Ash Wednesday. It is the one day of the church year when we celebrate our true beginning and acknowledge our death. It is good to look at the spirit God put into us, but we need to remember how he made us from dirt and water like a little mud pie that he shaped into his image and put his Holy Spirit into. I don't know why I'm wasting my time telling you things you should have learned years ago in catechism classes, but you ask such dumb questions."

"On Ash Wednesday the priest or his helper puts ashes on our head, the part of us that likes to think of itself as so smart and so superior. Do you know why the church in her wisdom chose to put the ashes on our forehead rather than our feet? He says, 'Remember, little one, you are dust and to dust you will return.'"

Mrs. Rodriquez was helping me to see our religion in a new light.

"Now if I was running the church, I would have made that a daily ritual because it's so important, but God realizes that when we see or hear something too often we no longer see or hear it at all. So the church in her wisdom gives us one special day every year to remind us who we are, where we came from and no matter how high we climb in our way where we're going to end up." She put a lid on the beans and turned off the fire.

"This could be my last Ash Wednesday, so I want to be home where they take it seriously. It's time to start seeing death as more than a friend, as my greatest benefactor, the easiest and surest door to heaven, the way to jump right into God's arms."

"Why, when my grandmother was my age, she was already home with God." She dried her hands on her apron. "My other grandmother, bless her heart, she never knew Jesus in this lifetime, but she loved his Father and I know the Father introduced her to the Son as soon as he had the chance. She never knew the blessings of the church but she loved the Great Spirit. And every morning as long as I can remember she greeted the sun with 'Today would be a great day to die.'" She poured herself a bowl of beans and one for me.

"It's time for me to long for the day I meet my Lord face to face. What kind of Christians are we if we're still afraid of death at my age? Look at the way Mother Teresa has made her peace with death. Why, she sees it as her best friend who will take her to her Beloved Spouse."

I joined her at the table.

"I love this beautiful world the good Lord made for me to practice with, so I wouldn't spoil the real one he has waiting for me. Saint Paul said when we were children we played with toys, but once we grew up we wanted something more fitting for adults. At my age it's time to get ready to enjoy the heavenly reality the Lord's been preparing for me even before he started making that little mud doll he shaped into me."

So Mrs. Rodriquez convinced me to take her to Uruapan, in Michoacán where she was born. We stayed at her second cousin's home.

On Ash Wednesday I saw what she meant about the biggest fiesta in her town. Every Catholic church in the village had people lined up to get ashes. "More people go to church on Ash Wednesday than on Easter or Christmas," Mrs. Rodriquez said.

We stood in the long line and the priest put ashes on our foreheads saying in Spanish, "Ashes to ashes and dust to dust. Remember, man, that thou art dust and to dust thou shall return."

In Uruapan Mrs. Rodriquez and I shared a bedroom. One night I woke up with a terrible cutting pain in my stomach. It terrified me, and I screamed waking her up.

"What's wrong?" she asked.

"I think I'm dying," I said dramatically. I really was afraid.

"If you're sick, I'll get up and care for you," she said, "but if you are really dying, that's between you and your Savior, and I'd just be in the way."

"I do feel I'm dying," I said. "I've never had such pain."

"Then work with your Savior," she said and turned over and went back to sleep. A few minutes later she was snoring. I wondered what Mother Teresa would have done if she'd been there.

I remembered how Mrs. Rodriquez had cared for me back in California when I was ill. She put me in bed, prayed over me and made me some "healing tea" with mint leaves she gathered from her garden. She had insisted I stay in bed, and all day she kept bringing me chicken soup, special teas and toast.

I suffered all night in Uruapan and begged God to take me quick if that was his plan and to heal me if I was to get well. I remembered how Mother Teresa always told us suffering was Jesus kissing us from the cross, getting so close he was sharing his redemptive suffering with us. When I woke up the next morning, I was still alive; in fact, my pain was gone. "Are you ready to start our voyage home?" Mrs. Rodriquez asked. "Thank you for taking me home for Ash Wednesday."

Whenever I was traveling, I would write to Mrs. Rodriquez, but she developed diabetes and lost her sight, and the young woman from Oaxaca who took care of her could not read, so the letters got ignored.

When I returned home and knocked on her door, Mrs. Rodriquez said, "Thank God, you are here, Maryanne. I thought you were dead. I said thirty rosaries to make sure you got out of purgatory and into heaven." That night Mrs. Rodriquez died. So now whenever I say a rosary, I remember to include her safe trip to heaven.

26

SICK AND SUFFERING COWORKERS

ONE MORNING I AWOKE TO FIND A HUGE BUMP OVER MY RIGHT EYE. A CT scan showed a life-threatening tumor in my head. My doctor assured me that the tumor was so rare many of the world's top neurosurgeons would be willing to operate, even for free if I could not afford them.

I was scheduled to spend the night in our church basement in a Coworker's program to shelter the homeless. I called my friend Irene, another Coworker, asking her to relieve me.

She believes in tough love: "Don't tell me you're going to desert the homeless just because you need an operation at some future date! I'm sorry you're sick, and I will pray for you every day. But your comfortable bed at home isn't going to be any better for you than a sleeping bag in the basement. In the church you will be too busy and have too many immediate problems to worry about your own. I will make your phone calls and tell everyone what food to bring. Get some rest so you will be ready to work tonight."

I did spend the night in the church basement, which was the best thing I could have done. It set the pattern for me to continue my life as close to normal as possible while I prepared for the brain surgery. And as Mother Teresa said, "The poor have so much to teach us. It is only when we get to heaven that we will realize how much the poor have given us."

That night a couple from San Salvador had a one-year-old baby who was in immediate danger of dying from pneumonia. Their problem made me forget my own, and I learned something about the poorest of the poor in America. Homeless people are not eligible for most official benefits because public assistance, most food programs and medical programs demand an address from each applicant. So one action we took was to find a temporary mailing address for all of the homeless people spending time with us.

Dr. Anita Figueredo, a medical doctor and the link for our Coworkers, suggested I go to the University of California at San Diego (UCSD) to see about my brain tumor. I had been volunteering as a translator for St. James medical missionaries, and they agreed with Dr. Figueredo.

I chose Dr. Hoi Sang U, a well-known neurosurgeon at UCSD. He said, "You have a very rare intraosseous meningioma and need surgery immediately. The tumor seems to be growing deeper into the brain."

I lay down on the table as he prepared a huge needle for a biopsy. "Lord, protect me from that awful thing," I prayed. The tumor was so hard the needle could not enter it at all. After several attempts Dr. U said, "We'll have to wait for the surgery to find out if it is malignant."

I wrote Jacqueline de Decker telling her that I wanted to be a Sick and Suffering Coworker. "Whenever I feel really sick, I find it hard to pray even though I feel an urgent need for prayers. So now while I can make a conscious decision, I want to offer all my pain to the Lord as Mother Teresa taught me. I want my life itself to be a prayer." Jacqueline's reply made me feel better about my operation. And being a Sick and Suffering Coworker gave me a sense of being close to Jesus and freed me of many of my fears.

Mother Teresa called suffering a gift from God–Jesus kissing us from his cross. Following her example, I turned to prayer for my healing: Mass, the Eucharist, rosaries and the Bible. I had all my friends and relatives praying for me and my name was on prayer lists all over the world.

Remembering the story of the Good Shepherd leaving ninety-nine sheep to look for one that was lost, I decided that God longs for the prayers of atheists. So I wrote my friend Mona, "I know you don't believe in God, but I do and you believe in me. I have a life-threatening tumor. Could you please pray for me?"

She wrote, "I was so moved by your letter I read it to my atheist friends and they agreed to help me pray. Some of us had prayed when we were children and they helped the rest of us find words. We prayed to Maryanne's God. We will keep praying as best we can. I hope this helps." (A few months later there was a huge earthquake in San Francisco where Mona and her friends lived. I bet they were glad they had some practice praying.)

I have never believed in surgery if there is any other possibility, so I went to St. Jude's clinic in Mexico where I tried all sorts of vitamins, minerals and nontraditional medicines. I went on a macrobiotic diet and lost thirty-five pounds. I felt wonderful but the bump on my head did not go down. I traveled to Hawaii to some native herbalists. At their suggestion I drank ocean water and tea made with red hibiscus.

At first my life was full of wild attempts to find a magic cure. Then I remembered how Mother Teresa said, "Everything is a gift from God. We must give him thanks." I realized that the illness had given me a new perspective on life. All the little material things that had seemed so important–bookkeeping, being on time, the tone someone used with me–no longer mattered. I began to see how precious life is and how ephemeral. Colors seemed more vivid. Cherry blossoms were sacred as were all things great and small. I was more alive to every moment. I hoped when my life was no longer held in suspension I would still feel so grateful to be alive.

My neurosurgeon begged me to set a date for the surgery. "The tumor has stopped growing," I said, "thanks to all the prayers and alternative treatments." He said, "The tumor is as large as a lemon and in a dangerous location." Still I procrastinated until I visited an eye specialist because I was having trouble with my sight. "You have a huge tumor wrapped around your optic nerve cutting off all the blood supply. I don't understand how you still have any vision in that eye," the specialist told me.

I called my neurosurgeon and scheduled the operation.

I had always thought of a brain operation as even worse than a heart operation. The doctors had to warn me I might be blind, paralyzed, lose some mental capacity or even die. Friends advised me to begin studying braille just in case.

For some reason I felt I would either go peacefully into the next life holding Jesus' hand or I would be completely well. After all, I was surrounded by love, by prayers from all nations, and even my atheist friends were praying for me.

When my surgeon explained that my head would have to be shaved, it was an obstacle that I hadn't expected. I thought about my friend Janet who had died of cancer. During her last months she refused to leave the house because her wigs kept sliding off her smooth bald head. I did not want to give up my hair. For days I cried and complained to my friends.

My son Raphael brought me some photos of glamorous women with bald heads. "See," he said. "They have style. These women cut off their hair because they feel you don't need hair to be beautiful. Beauty comes from within." He made a video of Sinead O'Connor. "See how great she looks," he said. "Your head is shaped just like hers. We will choose a whole new style of clothes for you that go with a bald head. You will look magnificent."

I was not yet ready to acknowledge his words of comfort. Was it my pride that refused to accept the baldness? Then I read how Mother Teresa and her nuns cut off their beautiful hair to become Missionaries of Charity. "Give Jesus anything he asks and take anything he gives with a smile," Mother advised us. And her example showed us how. Mother's words helped me to put aside my vanity and accept the inevitable.

The evening before my operation, we had a hair-styling party. My mother, my sister Susie and Raphael had come from Ohio to be with me during this time. Irene and some other Coworkers, including one friend named Lupe, joined us. We had some food and my friend and coworker Phyllis, a hairdresser, cut and arranged my hair in different styles before cutting it very short so that the shaving would not be so dramatic. We photographed each style. She promised to recreate my favorites as my hair grew back.

The surgery lasted ten hours and required five doctors. The plastic surgeon offered to throw in a free facelift. I said I'd take a raincheck.

The doctors expected me to spend several weeks in the hospital. I had collected books about Mother Teresa, inspirational photos and paintings to bring to the hospital. Dr. U advised me to have everything I wanted ready at home and have my family bring them when I got out of intensive care.

I left intensive care after one night and went home after five days.

When they took off the bandages and removed the stitches there was almost no scar. Every doctor who examined me afterward said, "It's a miracle how well you are healing." They had removed the top of my head and when I went to have the stitches out, the doctor said, "I've never seen anyone heal so rapidly."

My son took many photos of his beautiful bald mother. I learned that beauty does not come from any specific feature or accessory.

Beauty can come from without sometimes, from someone who loves us, from a cherry blossom tree, from a bird or an orchestra. If we will allow beauty to enter us, we will shine.

Of course there are many times when I take it all for granted, but my life is full of reminders of how blessed we all are to share this sacred planet, how nature serenades us each day, how God is in love with each of us.

A few weeks after the operation, I was able to return to work as a Coworker of Mother Teresa.

Each year I go for a CT scan to make certain no tumors have returned. Last year Dr. U told me, "Maryanne, your surgery helped to save the life of a young athlete. His tumor was identical to yours. That was the first time I've seen such a rare tumor twice. But with the knowledge I had from operating on you, I knew exactly what I was doing. It was a piece of cake. So not only did we heal you, we healed that young man."

27

GLIMPSES OF MOTHER TERESA

WHEN I WENT TO OHIO TO VISIT MY FAMILY, MY NINE-YEAR-OLD NIECE Courtney shouted, "Your Mother Teresa is famous!"

"Yes, I know. She won the Nobel Peace Prize!"

"It's better than that," Courtney said. "She's on MTV with Michael Jackson!"

A short time later, she called me to watch a video of Michael singing about the man in the mirror while movie clips were shown, among them Mother Teresa in Ethiopia.

I will never forget the time the University of San Diego awarded Mother Teresa an honorary doctorate. The mayor of San Diego gave Mother the key to the city and asked, "Why would she want the key to any city when she has the key to heaven?"

During the entire preliminary session Mother sat on the stage saying her rosary. As they introduced her, describing her many achievements, Mother never stopped praying. "And here she is: Mother Teresa!" Mother went on fingering her beads.

"Mother Teresa of Calcutta!"

The crowd applauded and everyone stood up. Mother continued praying her rosary. Finally someone walked over to her. "Mother, it's your turn to talk."

Mother put away her rosary, walked up to the mic and spoke to us with the same intensity and concentration she had put into her prayers. She spoke about how Mary hurried to Elizabeth when the angel Gabriel told her they were both with child. And she asked, "Are you taking Jesus to others?" She reminded us that it was the unborn child, Saint John, who was the first to recognize Jesus while they were both in the womb.

While I began my book for young adults, I decided to write it for people of all ages since Mother's spirit touches all of us.

When Mother Teresa came to Tijuana to celebrate the ordination of a Polish brother who was becoming a priest, some of us Coworkers spent the night at the hostel of the Missionaries of Charity. That night my friend Lupe and I sat talking with other Coworkers when suddenly the lights went out. Someone shouted, "Who turned out the lights?"

"I did," Mother Teresa said. "Girls, girls, tomorrow we have a big day. It's already nine o'clock and we can't waste so much electricity." Now whenever I leave the lights on too long, I think of Mother coming to turn them off, and I find myself following her example.

The next morning we attended the ordination. As always when Mother Teresa visited a location, the seminary in Tijuana was overflowing with people.

When it was over, we Coworkers waited outside the building to talk with Mother Teresa. Inside Mother met with her sisters. Someone opened the window next to where I stood. It was as though I had been invited to share Mother's private moment with her sisters. Every time Mother said something the sisters laughed with joy. There was something so mystical about Mother's voice and the nuns' laughter that I found myself feeling high. It felt like Mother was speaking to my heart rather than my mind.

I remember thinking, "They remind me of Zen Koans, puzzles

that Buddhist masters use to teach their students, sentences like 'What is the sound of one hand clapping?'"

But Mother offered no puzzles. She was expressing her joy at seeing her sisters. I understood or thought I understood every word Mother said. But immediately afterward as the sisters laughed, I forgot everything, and my mind was a complete blissful blank.

My eyes were focused on the door to the building. At any moment someone would invite us Coworkers to join Mother.

I felt someone squeeze my hand. I looked around but didn't see anyone. Then I glanced down and there was Mother Teresa. Her head barely reached my chest. The skin of her hand was rough like a laborer's, but her energy was tender and uplifting. Warmth flooded my body. I knew she was praying for me. I thought, "This is like holding hands with Jesus." Never before had I felt such happiness, a deep peace with joyful excitement.

Kissing a miraculous medal, Mother lovingly put it in my hand, closed my fingers into a fist and patted my fist. I could not believe this was real. While she was standing next to me, Madre Antonia, another living saint, approached us. She lived voluntarily in a prison in Tijuana helping all the prisoners. "I love you, Mother Teresa," she said.

"Then pray for me. Pray that I won't spoil the work."

"Oh, I do, Mother," Madre Antonia said. I felt so blessed to be next to two holy women.

A huge monk came out of the building and called, "Please come back inside, Mother. It isn't safe out here!" He tried to hold onto her, but she squirmed out of his hands and seemed to dive into the crowd, continuing to kiss medals and pass them out.

The memories of the precious days I spent with Mother Teresa will always remain in my mind. Once we had a meeting at Dr. Figueredo's house and a Coworker offered a washer and dryer for the sisters in Tijuana who were caring for many babies in diapers.

We found a truck and when we arrived, Mother said, "No thank you. The sisters don't need these. They want to live like the poor around them."

So we prayed about it. Lupe and I asked God to show us what to do with the washer and dryer. Many Mexican people kept asking about it. But most of them did not have water or electricity.

Finally a lady with five children who had water and electricity asked for the washer and dryer. We decided the Holy Spirit wanted her to have it. Mother had said, "Give it to the person who needs it most." We knew God intended the machine for her family and had used us as his instruments.

One day Irene and I went to work at the soup kitchen in Tijuana. The sisters were so happy to see us they asked us to prepare the lunch while they prayed. We had to pick out the edible green beans from a huge barrel of rotten beans. There was no other food but rice and bread and there were many people to feed. As we worked with the bad-smelling beans, I thought of how Mother Teresa ignored bad smells when she cared for wounded human beings. We managed to get enough good beans to make a delicious dish. When the food was ready, a large crowd gathered and everyone seemed to enjoy it. Irene and I had lost our appetites, but we were glad to see our work was appreciated.

Mother Teresa sent me a beautiful letter for my fiftieth birthday, wishing me fifty more years to serve the Lord in my neighbor and in God's beloved poor.

A friend asked me, "What was Mother Teresa really like? Was she as serious as she appears in photos?" That question shocked me because in the photos I have of Mother she is happy. I remember her laughing or smiling most of the time. Having a good sense of humor is an important requirement for being a Missionary of Charity. "The poor have enough sorrow," Mother said. "We must bring them joy."

I'm often asked how working with Mother Teresa changed my life. Completely. I went from a lukewarm cradle Catholic to a daily communicant with a radical faith in God. Mother Teresa said, "Never worry about money. God gives us enough money for anything he wants us to do." Mother took care of thousands of people and turned all her would-be worries over to God.

At first I thought, "That's fine for you, Mother Teresa. You're a saint. Of course, God takes care of you, but I'm a single parent with health problems. I have to look out for my son and myself." After spending time with Mother Teresa, I learned that God is always there for Raphael and me with the same tender love he showed Mother. I believe Mother was right when she said, "We need to trust God and know that he will see to all our needs."

Do I Have to Go to Heaven?

Mother Teresa encouraged us to be devoted to Jesus' Sacred Heart. My Grandma Patterson used to say, "The family that worships the Sacred Heart is blessed with happy death."

I asked her, "What is a happy death?"

"Any death that brings us home to God," she said.

On July 4, 1995, I learned my father had a malignant brain tumor. Earlier he had told me, "When I was little, I wasn't afraid of death. I knew I'd go to heaven. I don't believe in God or in heaven anymore, but I've seen hell, and I'm afraid to spend eternity there." My family and friends and I prayed for Dad. I asked the shepherds of Fatima to beg God to restore his faith.

On October 14 my sister Susie called, "Daddy is dying. If you want to come home, we'll buy your ticket." During the long flight, I thought of Mother Teresa's words about a happy death, and I prayed for Daddy. I also prayed to arrive in time for another good-bye.

When I saw my father, he was unconscious. The family surrounded him, wiping his brow, covering him, touching him. We stayed close to each other. In death's presence, every relationship is precious.

Everyone was exhausted after spending the last forty-eight hours with Dad. My brother Tom and I spent Saturday night with him. He was semi-conscious, very thirsty but unable to drink. I kept thinking of all of Mother Teresa's chapels with "I Thirst" and how Jesus was so thirsty on the cross. Mother explained to us that Jesus' real thirst was for souls. I felt Daddy's thirst was for God. Tom and I took turns putting wet sponges in Daddy's mouth. I kept thinking of the bitter sponge Jesus was given to drink before he died.

We said rosaries all night. I told Tom how Mother Teresa loved the rosary, how she had her sisters counting distance traveled by how many rosaries they said on the road.

Around 3:00 AM Daddy groaned. He woke up and asked, "Do I have to go to heaven?"

"If you get an invitation, take it," Tom said. I thought Daddy was asking if he had to die, but I was relieved because I was convinced he believed in heaven again.

Just as Mother Teresa's words about death consoled me when my brother John died, they helped me when my father was dying. I told Dad about Mother Teresa giving the dying a ticket to Saint Peter. When the priest came to see my father, he went to confession and took Communion, and we all said a rosary.

On Sunday, nobody wanted to leave Daddy to go to Mass. Around 2:00 PM the nurses asked us to leave the room while they examined Daddy. "That's not necessary," my sister Susie, a nurse, said. "You won't have to do that again." The nurses left.

Mother sat on Daddy's bed. "It's OK, Vince." I had never seen my mother so in control of herself or of the scene. She was regal. "You can stop fighting. Johnny is waiting. And your sister Kathleen. Your brother Charles. Your mom and dad. You can go home now."

I remembered Raffie, a Yorkie puppy I loved that had died recently. "Raffie, lead Daddy home," I said through my tears. "And there's Kathy's cat," my six-year-old niece said. "Alex, help Raffie take Grandpa to heaven!"

The moment was magic. Most of Dad's ten children were there

and many grandchildren, including unborn Kelsy who arrived five days after Daddy died.

The invisible curtain separating heaven and earth opened. It seemed possible to see all our beloved dead, but my attention was with my immediate family saying good-bye to Daddy. He was semiconscious but he opened his eyes and his expression was ecstatic. I had never seen him so happy. He reached out, then fell back silent.

"He's gone." Susie set the time of death with her watch. Dad had often asked the nurses for his watch, so I knew it was important to him. "Can I have Dad's watch?" I asked.

"It's a man's watch," one of my brothers said.

"I'm the oldest. If God wanted a man to have the watch, he would have made our oldest male."

Susie handed me the watch, and I put it on, and I still wear it today. It reminds me to pray often for Daddy's soul. We sat with Daddy until the ambulance came. I wrote in my journal. My niece Courtney asked, "What are you doing?"

"Writing about Daddy."

"Can I read it?"

After reading my entry, she asked if she could write in the book. When Courtney finished, she showed what she had written to her mother. Soon everybody was reading and writing in my journal. I was embarrassed that they were seeing my most private thoughts because I had a habit of complaining in my journal. But the shared diary helped us feel together during an intense time.

I know Mother Teresa would have shared our happiness.

Being with my family at Daddy's death, witnessing the joy and peace on his face, erased the grief I had expected. I shared his peace. The prayers for a happy death had been heard.

Later whenever someone said, "I'm sorry about your father," I almost said, "Don't be sorry. Rejoice. He believed in heaven when he died, and he accepted God's invitation."

29

Mother Teresa Goes Home to God

In 1992 Mother Teresa was admitted to Scripps Hospital in La Jolla, California. She stayed in the hospital for a long time. Dr. Anita Figueredo, link for the Coworkers in southwest United States and Dr. Patricia Aubanel, a cardiologist, looked after her. Some Coworkers went to the hospital. The doctors told us that she was critical. We went into the chapel and prayed.

After Mother Teresa was released from the hospital, she spent Christmas in El Florido, the children's home in Mexico. We Coworkers worried about Mother since we went to the children's home on a regular basis and knew the situation.

The weather was cold and there was no heat in the home. There was no running water, very limited amount of drinking water, and the children had lots of colds and fevers. We were afraid Mother would catch a children's disease if she didn't freeze to death first.

We could understand why Mother would go there–the sisters' smiles and the children running up to her for hugs. Mother survived the Mexican Children's Home and had a joyful Christmas.

Mother sent me a note thanking me for my prayers:

Dear Maryanne,
With deep appreciation I thank you for remembering me in your prayers. My gratitude will be my prayer for you that you may

become humble like Mary so as to become more and more like Jesus. Together, let us thank God for all His tender love and care. He has been so good to me.

The care that I received while in the hospital has been something great and beautiful. I am spoiled. Now that I have left the hospital and am feeling better, I ask you to pray much for China. We have been invited to bring Jesus to the people there who are hungering so much for God. Continue to pray for me and my sisters that we may not spoil God's work. Always be one heart full of love in the hearts of Jesus and Mary.

God bless you,

M. Teresa, M. C.

If anyone ever deserved to be spoiled, it was Mother Teresa who gave the poor for love what the rich receive for money.

When she left California, Mother went to Albania for the first time and opened a house in Tirana where her own mother and sister had died.

I remained in southern California praying with the Coworkers, helping out at the soup kitchen in Tijuana, bringing clothes and holding the babies in the orphanage at El Florido. I continued writing my book.

In August 1997 my friend Irene Nicolai took me home with her to South Africa to see her father who was ill. We made arrangements to visit the Missionaries of Charity. Early Sunday morning, August 31, 1997, Mother's friend Princess Diana was killed in an automobile accident in Paris. Mother Teresa made a public statement: "She was in love with the poor, anxious to do something for them. That is why we were so close. All the sisters and I are praying for her and all the members of the family. May they know God's speed and peace and comfort in this moment."

Five days later, on the evening of September 5, Irene's father and I were watching a program about the death of Princess Diana when a special bulletin announced that Mother Teresa had just died. For me the most difficult part of watching Diana's funeral was hearing the choir sing Mother Teresa's favorite, the peace prayer of Saint Francis.

I cried for Mother and for Princess Diana. Not really for them, but for we who had lost them. It seemed strange that Mother Teresa and Princess Diana who loved and admired one another should both die within such a short time of each other.

When Irene and I went to the bakery the next day, everyone was talking about Mother Teresa's death. A young girl who worked there said, "I met Mother Teresa once at the airport. She held my hand and smiled at me. I'll never forget her smile or the way I felt when I was with her. I'm so blessed!" I knew what she meant.

The next day the sisters called to say they had been invited to parliament. The national assembly passed a resolution expressing its sorrow at the death of Mother Teresa, paying tribute to her and offering its condolences. The sisters asked us to meet them at the archbishop's home when they left parliament. They invited us to go home with them. Father Curran, their pastor, drove us there. As we traveled into the countryside outside of Cape Town, we celebrated Mother's heavenly joy and mourned our earthly loss. We tried to focus on the joy, but all of us found tears rolling down our faces.

I asked the sisters if getting rid of the racist government and apartheid had affected their work. "Not at all," the sisters agreed. "We never had any separation here. Our sisters come from all countries, all different races, and we care for anyone who needs us, no matter who they are. We are all God's children and we see God in each person."

30

My Trip to India

Ever since I first read about Mother Teresa and Calcutta, I dreamed of going there. I prayed about it, but I had to settle for finding my own Calcutta wherever I was. Then my son Raphael and his wife, Ginger, got work teaching at the American embassy in New Delhi. On November 17, 2000, they had a child, my first grandchild, Zeal.

In April 2001 I was able to go to India to visit my family. I made plans to spend time in New Delhi and in Calcutta. Shortly before I left, I met Cindy Perez, a lay missionary of Mother Teresa who had also been praying to visit Calcutta. We decided to travel together. She would spend all of her time with the Missionaries of Charity, and I would spend most of mine with my son and his family.

Raphael met us at the airport in New Delhi. My suitcase had been lost, so I had to buy some Indian clothes to wear. Raphael took us to his home at the embassy, where we spent the night. The next morning Cindy went to work with the Missionary of Charity sisters in Delhi.

A few days after we arrived in New Delhi, I got a phone call from Father Damian, a Missionaries of Charity priest who was a good friend of mine when he lived at the seminary in Tijuana. He used to tell me when Mother Teresa was coming to Mexico or California.

We corresponded for years, but I had not heard from him for over a year. He had run into Cindy, and she gave him my son's phone number.

Father Damian was the first of Mother's Missionaries of Charity brothers. Mother had asked him to join the brothers so they would have their own priest. He was in Calcutta with Mother for twenty-five years.

The next morning Father Damian came for me in an old Missionaries of Charity ambulance. He took me to Mother Teresa's Home for Abandoned Boys where he lived. Cindy joined us for a tour of the house. Father introduced us to the children. At lunch time he gave us a plate of rice and dal. We laughed about the time we were at the Tijuana seminary when both Father and I were on crutches and everyone joked about our unsuccessful ski trip.

After I spent a day with Father and his boys, he arranged for some seminarians to drive me home since they were taking the ambulance to an embassy near Raphael's home.

On the way home the ambulance suddenly stopped in the middle of the road. Everyone who was near us came running to help push the ambulance. They loved Mother and recognized her vehicle. I was thankful we did not have a patient with a heart attack.

Cindy and I took a train from New Delhi to Calcutta. We wanted to go the cheapest class the way Mother's sisters travel, but my son insisted we go first class. He said women don't travel without a man on a train in India so we would be safer that way.

We had a sleeper car large enough for four people; we were surprised when two Indian gentlemen joined us, but we each had our own sleeper and a little curtain to close.

Our food was included in the price of our tickets, but I was disappointed to learn that they only served European food in first class. When I asked for Indian food–rice and curried vegetables–I was told that is served only in second class. I finally talked them into giving me Indian food.

As the train rushed through the night, I looked out the window and thought of Mother Teresa's train to Darjeeling when she received her second call. I remembered how she said the most important thing we could do was have an encounter with Jesus, a conversion when we see ourselves in his eyes, see the unconditional, all-consuming love he has for us and fall in love with him. This experience would enable us to surrender our lives, to do what he asked and give what he requested with a smile. Otherwise, without the encounter, we can burn out when we try to do his work. She often said that her own encounter with Jesus on the train to Darjeeling gave her the strength and courage to do God's will no matter what it was. I prayed for such an encounter.

I had told Agnes Gomes I was coming to Calcutta by train. She wanted the details and said she might have friends who could pick us up. Since we did not know Calcutta and did not have much money, we were happy at the possibility.

The train ride lasted five hours. When the train stopped and everyone started leaving, we asked the conductor, "Is this Calcutta?" He said, "This is Houghly Station. We are a couple of miles from Calcutta."

So we began preparing our bags. Everyone got out. The air conditioning stopped. We seemed to be the only ones left in the train. We decided to step outside and see what was happening.

There was Agnes Gomes and her helpers with a large sign that read: "Maryanne Raphael, Coworker of Mother Teresa." Agnes was about the same size as Mother Teresa and looked about her age. She was dressed in a brown sari.

"We almost left," she said. "We decided to say one more rosary and then to give up. Thank God we said that last rosary. Just as we finished you came out of the train."

Agnes picked us up in a Missionaries of Charity ambulance. The driver took us directly to the children's home where we met Sister Monica, the sister in charge. I had a photo taken with Sister Monica on one side and Agnes on the other, and behind us a painting of Mother Teresa saving drowning people. Sister Monica held up a copy of my book that I had given her.

Although I did not want to bother Sister Nirmala, Agnes insisted that we go to the motherhouse so she could find a place for us. Sister Nirmala was busy, so I asked another sister where we could find a room and she suggested we stay at the hotel across the street. The hotel had two price lists: A room with air conditioning starting at one hundred dollars per night, one without was ten dollars. In spite of the intense heat, we paid ten dollars for our room.

Thousands of people lived their entire lives in the streets of Calcutta. That first morning I wondered why they were covered with burlap when it was so hot. I was told they had died during the night.

We heard Mass at the motherhouse. A statue of Mother at prayer with Sister Nirmala made it easy to feel she was still there with us.

After Mass we gathered for a cookie and some fruit punch. Then a group of us headed for the home for the dying. We went together in a crowded city bus, most of us standing at the back of the bus.

The sign over the door read: "Corporation of Calcutta Nirmal Hriday, Home for Dying Destitutes." The house had two large rooms, one for women, one for men. It was attached to the temple of Kali on the banks of a stream. Men and women lay on cots. Many were unconscious or semiconscious.

It was a strange déjà vu for me. I felt as though I had lived Mother's life since I had spent so much time researching it. Although this was my first trip to Calcutta, I felt as though I had spent many years here. Many pilgrims came here. People died peacefully in this sacred place. There was no bustle around the dying. The only sounds were soft whispers, death rattles, sounds from the street and rice boiling.

I stepped inside. I was getting used to the dim light when a woman lying on a cot grabbed hold of my pant leg and began pulling. She was shouting in an Indian dialect that I could not understand. The woman next to her began to translate. "She needs your assistance. She has to go to the toilet, but she is blind and very weak. She can't go alone, but she needs to go right away."

Having just entered the room, I had no idea where the toilet was or what the practice was for getting a dying patient there. But the two women were insistent. The one kept pulling at me and the other kept telling me how urgent it was. I got the woman out of bed and helped her walk toward the back of the huge room, careful to avoid tripping over other cots. I asked several volunteers for directions, but like me they were new.

All of the sisters were busy with other people with even more urgent needs. So I kept walking, holding my lady up. She kept tugging at me. Finally a sister showed us the toilet, a series of simple holes in the ground. I held my lady up while she went to the bathroom. The sister said we must give her a bath while she is up. So she began washing her. The lady held on to me as though I were her lifeline. She refused to let go at anytime while the sister was washing her. When she was clean and dry, sister gave her a clean dress and then I helped her back to her bed.

I started to help her into bed, but I was told, "Wait, her cot is wet. You must get her a clean mattress." She pointed to where they were stacked. When I had put it in place, she told me I must turn it over. "The wrong side is up." So I turned the mattress over, and finally my lady was able to lie back down and get comfortable in her little bed.

I went from bed to bed greeting the sick and dying patients although some were unconscious and many did not speak English. But most showed some sign of appreciation, reaching for my hand, smiling or saying something.

I had been eager to visit the home for the dying in Calcutta. A sign on the wall said: "Mother's First Love." Malcolm Muggeridge had described the home for the dying as a mystical holy home with miraculous light that shone in the darkness. I think that is how many people think of Mother Teresa, part of a miracle. To me, Mother was a not miracle, but a special, down-to-earth human being who touched the face of God.

Finally, Cindy and I went to Agnes Gomes's home where Mother Teresa started her order. Agnes still lives there and has now moved into the upper floor where Mother Teresa and her first twelve sisters lived. It was thrilling to be in the beautiful old house. There was a picture of Gandhi on the wall along with several saints' pictures and the picture of Our Lady that Mother had over the chapel when she lived there. We felt so blessed to be able to spend time in this holy place.

Before I left Calcutta, I visited Mother's tomb at the mother-house. I prayed and thanked God for giving us Mother Teresa, and I thanked her for enriching my life, for teaching me how to love God with my whole heart and mind and soul and to see him and love him in my neighbor.

I thanked her for teaching me how to write from the heart. She once asked a man who gave speeches about poverty, "If you don't know any poor people, how can you know their needs?" I had always felt writing was my mission and had no compulsion to do any other service. Mother taught me that if I was to write about "her work" I would have to get in there and get my hands dirty. I became an active Coworker. I helped in soup kitchens, changed diapers and fed babies in children's shelters, cared for and comforted the sick, elderly and poor.

Mother taught me without love there is no passion or compassion. Without love, life has no meaning. Mother wanted everyone to know God's love and to love God as she did. She told us we are all called to love one another as our Father loves us and she showed us how.

31

BLESSED MOTHER TERESA

FOUR YEARS AFTER MOTHER DIED, WHEN THE CHURCH WAS INVESTIGATING her life for potential sainthood, a secret she had hidden was revealed. Mother Teresa had gone through a feeling of abandonment from the beginning of her work in the slums until her death. Because she believed we must smile at those we help and encourage one another with joy and smiles, she hid her own suffering.

Her trial of faith seems to be what John of the Cross, a sixteenth-century Spanish saint, described as the "dark night of the soul."

Saint Thérèse, the Little Flower, Mother's patron saint, wrote of her trial of faith in her autobiography. It was similar to Mother's, and both struggled to be light to others even from the darkest night. In a time of great doubt, Saint Thérèse wrote poems of praise describing what she wanted to believe: "I believe the demon has asked God's permission to tempt me with extreme suffering to make me fail in patience and faith. The pain is so bad one could easily take one's life."

Mother wrote letters to her spiritual advisers showing painful spiritual struggles during the 1950s. She said, "At times I feel like an empty vessel, a limp rag. I feel so alone, so miserable."

The sensation was difficult for Mother after her intense encounter with Jesus on the train to Darjeeling. "I want God with all my soul and yet there is a terrible separation. Heaven from every side is closed. I feel that terrible pain of loss, of God not wanting me, of God not being God, of God not really existing. These thoughts return like sharp knives and hurt my soul."

Mother thought how Jesus felt abandoned on the cross when he cried, "My God, my God, why have you forsaken me?" (Matthew 27:46).

Jesus had said to Mother, "I want to use you for my glory. Wilt thou refuse?" Even in the darkest night, the most sterile moment, she never refused him. Even when she doubted his very existence, she cried out, "Yes, Jesus, yes!" Part of her message was that we don't have to feel the emotion of love to live it.

Mother Teresa and the archbishop of Calcutta, Henry D'Souza, were in the same hospital. Mother Teresa was suffering from problems with her heart. She was calm during the day but at night she appeared extremely agitated, pulling off wires and other monitors stuck to her body.

The archbishop felt Mother might be under attack from the Evil One, and offered to arrange an exorcism. She said, "I am so small I don't think the devil would bother with me, but I want to do whatever you feel is best."

After it was over, mother slept like a baby.

Certain scholars have suggested Mother will become the patron saint of the lonely, unwanted and unloved.

In the Middle Ages, when a very holy person died, the local church could canonize them. Francis of Assisi, who, like Mother Teresa chose to live in poverty and care for lepers and the poor, was canonized only two years after his death. Cardinal Joseph Ratzinger, now Pope Benedict XVI, said, "Because her life was so resplendent before the eyes of everybody, her cause will not present many problems, so I don't think too long a process will be necessary."

Pope John Paul II waived the traditional five-year waiting period before beginning and expedited the process. Since the Holy Father and Mother Teresa were such close friends, he was well aware of her holiness. "She will be a saint," he promised.

Twelve investigators began studying Mother's life on July 26, 1999. After the investigation was completed, she was declared venerable because they were satisfied that she led an exemplary life.

Next a miracle was required. An Indian woman, Monika Besra, had a tumor declared incurable. She asked Mother's sisters to pray for her. They prayed and put a medal Mother had kissed on her stomach, and she was healed. Doctors declared it miraculous, and Mother Teresa was beatified and called blessed.

Now she needs another miracle to be canonized, which means the church declares that she is with God and her life is an example for us. She then has the title saint.

Although everyone knew Mother Teresa would one day be canonized, we Coworkers were excited when the Holy Father decided on a shortcut to her cause. We followed the articles in the newspapers about the progress.

When it was announced that Mother Teresa would be beatified in October 2003, I began praying to be able to attend. Mother Teresa always said nothing was impossible with God. I believed God could get me there; I hoped it was his will.

Dr. Anita Figueredo, the director of Coworkers in the southwestern United States, organized a group of Coworkers and friends of Mother Teresa to go to Rome. She was one of the witnesses called to testify in the canonization process. And she was one of the ten people chosen in advance to receive Communion directly from the Holy Father, honored for their longtime friendship and work with Mother.

Many years ago when Dr. Figueredo's eighteen-month-old son Bobby died in an accident, Mother Teresa made Bobby the patron of the Missionaries of Charity brothers, someone close to God who could help them.

I did not sign up to go with Dr. Figueredo because a friend got me a standby ticket to Rome for less than half-price. However, I soon learned I would have to go weeks early while there were seats. But when I checked on the hotel prices it was less expensive to buy a regular ticket. By that time I couldn't find a plane reservation to arrive for the beatification.

After many prayers and phone calls one of Mother's sisters connected me with Catholic Travel, and I was able to fly with them to Rome where we took a train to Assisi, the medieval city where Saints Francis and Clare lived.

We were also at the Vatican for Pope John Paul II's twenty-fifth anniversary Mass, a few days before Mother's beatification.

Mother Teresa's order has opened 72 centers worldwide, with 4,000 members in 125 countries. Her Missionaries feed 500,000 families a year in Calcutta alone, treat 90,000 leprosy patients annually and educate 20,000 children every year.

When Mother Teresa was on earth, the Secretary General of the United Nations called her "the most powerful woman in the world." Sister Nirmala says now Mother is with God and she is much more powerful than she was on earth.

For a short time in the history of eternity an angel touched the earth. I was blessed to spend precious days with her. I feel a little more at home, a little better for having shared the world with a saint.

Mother Teresa inspired me to love my own family, my neighborhood, my town passionately seeing God in everyone. She helped me be a better mother for my son whom I was raising alone. Following her example and her words, "Love begins at home," I learned to listen to my son, to be more understanding, considerate and loving. We grew closer.

Her all-consuming love for humanity helped me truly love the world. She said, "Do not believe that love to be true must be extraordinary." She taught me to love Jesus in all I meet, to smile at him in a person who is angry, boring or irritating. She taught me to be ready to forgive at all times, for how could I stay angry at Jesus no matter his disguise?

Mother often spoke of how perfect love cast out fear, and she helped me conquer my fear of death, to see death as the way home. I remember Mother saying good-bye to a little boy who was dying of AIDS. "Here's your ticket to Saint Peter." She smiled as she hugged him, kissed his cheek and said, "Now when you see Jesus and his mother Mary, give them my love. Tell them I am coming home as soon as they are ready for me." Watching Mother, you would have thought he was going to camp or to visit a favorite relative.

Mother's love for life was an uncut quilt. She taught me to love life wherever I found it, in an unborn child, a person with Hanson's disease, a condemned murderer, someone with AIDS, someone taking his last breath. She often ended her talks with, "It's not how much we do, it's how much love we put into it." My goal is to put some of Mother Teresa's unconditional love into everything I do.

Epilogue

Every century or two, when darkness threatens humanity, God sends a holy person to light our way, reminding us of his unconditional love and his longing for humankind to love him in one another. We who shared the earth with Mother Teresa were blessed in many ways. She inspired us with her great compassion, her enormous love for the poor, the leper, the condemned killer, the dying.

Mother Teresa was the world's conscience. She was the symbol of love, faithfulness and goodness. Knowing she was in the world gave us a feeling of security.

The Bible tells how Abraham asked God if he would spare a certain wicked city if there were ten good men living there. God said, "I will spare it if I can find one." As long as Mother Teresa was in our world, we knew that God could find at least one good soul.

Mother has been gone a while now, and the world recognizes the great loss. Brother Angelo Devananda, who helped Mother start a contemplative order for men, said, "When the time comes for Mother to leave us it will be the real heart and spiritual vision of her life that will endure and shine brightly in the midst of our world's uncertainty. Mother was a true teacher whose desire was to point beyond, and then to disappear."

But in a deeper sense Mother is still here. Mother's patron saint, the Little Flower, Saint Thérèse of Lisieux, promised on her deathbed, "I will spend my heaven doing good for those on earth."

Jesus said, "Know that I am with you always." Mother Teresa, who followed Jesus and Saint Thérèse so closely, will surely do the same.

Mother's sisters, brothers, priests and Coworkers continue helping the world's impoverished people. She left over 4,500 nuns in 585 houses in over 120 countries. Her personal touch and global vision have inspired many. When people asked Mother what would happen to her order once she died, she said, "God will find someone to do the work. I'm only an instrument in God's hands. It is his work. He will see that it continues."

On November 24, 1998, Sister Nirmala wrote these words to her Coworkers, both active and sick and suffering: "Please pray for me and for all our sisters, especially the ninety-five who will make their first vows and seventy-seven who will make their final vows in different parts of the world this December."

"You will be very happy to know that since Mother's going home to Jesus, we have been able to offer Jesus twenty new tabernacles all around the world, and after the profession in December, we are offering him another fifteen new tabernacles."

At the speed the Missionaries of Charity order is growing, the world can expect it to survive.

The sisters bring God's love and joy to everyone. The Coworkers gather once a month for prayer, adoration of the Blessed Sacrament or Mass and do what they can about neighborhood problems. They may work with the Missionaries of Charity in their soup kitchens, orphanages or hospices. They visit AIDS patients, gather blankets for the homeless, have parties for poor and sick children.

One reason Mother's Missionaries of Charity have few problems continuing without her is the fact that the various international homes ran on their own even while Mother was alive. Mother was only able to visit many homes a few times, so they were already used to operating without her physical presence.

The Holy Father began the year 2000 with what he called a "Vatican Woodstock." He invited children from all over the world and sponsored a concert right outside his window. He invited Sister Nirmala to speak to them. The sisters' warm relationship with the Holy Father is one reason the Missionaries of Charity have continued to thrive.

Sister Nirmala has said, "We are determined the work will go on. We, Mother's sisters, know the best tribute we can give her is continuing what she taught us with her life and her example, wherever we are."

Some people wanted to call her Mother now that she is the head of the order, Sister Nirmala said, "No, Mother Teresa is our Mother."

One problem facing Mother's order is the fact that many Christians are being tortured for their faith today. Father A.T. Thomas, a Jesuit priest, was beheaded in Bihar, India, on October 28, 1997. Not long afterward robbers stole a truck carrying food and medicine from Calcutta to Mother Teresa's home in Patna. They killed Missionaries of Charity Brother Luke Puttaniyil and the two volunteers who were with him.

In January of 1998 Missionaries of Charity sisters were held hostage in Freetown, Sierra Leone. Three were shot and killed. Four were released, including the wounded Sister Indu, a Xaverian Missionary brother, and two other hostages. Sister Indu died one week after being released. Three more sisters were shot and died in Hodieda, Yemen, in July of 1998 while leaving their convent on their way to work in their soup kitchen.

In her November 1998 letter to the Coworkers, Sister Nirmala wrote: "Our seven sisters went home to Jesus in little over one month this year. Mother seems to be gathering many more intercessors around her to pray for us. Let us pray for them and ask them to pray for us."

Mother Teresa surrendered her life to her God and became "a pencil in his hands so he could write his love letter to the world." Today that letter is still being written, in the form of Mother Teresa's Coworkers and Missionaries, who affect the lives of over four million people. What began as one tiny nun's relationship with Jesus has spread all over the world.

To her, all life was precious. She would have given her own life to save an unborn baby or a convicted serial killer condemned to capital punishment. She saw Jesus in everyone. She felt the whole world's pain, heard the afflicted crying in the night and rushed to comfort them.

Once she met Jesus, she never took her eyes off him. He wasn't, as Mother often said, always easy to please, but he kept his promises and she could count on him to fill her life with miracles when she needed them most. By being God's instrument of love, peace and healing, she showed the world what one human being can do, how one can work through God, with whom all things are possible.

"We are all called to love," Mother Teresa said, and the example of her life reminds us that the future of humanity depends on whether we are listening.

Bibliography

Accurso, Lina. "What Mother Teresa Means to Me." *Liguorian,* February 1983, p. 17.

Bang, Kirsten. *Yougga Finds Mother Teresa,* Kathryn Spink, trans. Tisbury, Wiltshire: Element, 1983.

Bethell, Tom. "Mother Teresa's Sisters Help AIDS Victims," *Catholic Digest,* January 1987, p. 36.

Chetcuti, Paul. *Choosing to Serve the Destitute,* Michael P. Gallagher, trans. Irish Messenger Publications, 1980.

Cocagnac, A.M, and Rosemary Haughton, eds., *Bible for Young Christians.* New York: MacMillan, 1966.

Conroy, Susan. *Mother Teresa's Lessons of Love and Secrets of Sanctity.* Huntington, Ind.: Our Sunday Visitor, 2003.

——. *Praying In The Presence of Our Lord With Mother Teresa.* Huntington, Ind.: Our Sunday Visitor, 2005.

Constant, Audrey. *In the Streets of Calcutta: The Story of Mother Teresa.* London: Pergamon, 1980.

Craig, Mary. *Mother Teresa.* London: Hamilton Children's Books, 1983.

Day, Dorothy. *Therese.* Springfield, Ill.: Templegate, 1979.

Doig, Desmond. *Mother Teresa, Her People and Her Work.* San Francisco: Harper and Row, 1976.

Eagan, Eileen. "Mother Teresa, The Myth and the Person." *America,* March 22, 1980.

——. "Mother Teresa," *Saints Are Now.* John Delaney, ed. Garden City, N.Y.: Image, 1983.

——. *Such a Vision of the Streets.* Garden City, N.Y.: Doubleday, 1986.

Fisher, Louis. *The Life of Mahatma Gandhi.* New York: Harper and Row, 1950.

Gasnick, Roy M., O.F.M. *The Francis Book.* New York: Macmillan, 1980.

——. "The World's Most Popular Saint." *Catholic Digest,* November 1982, p. 57.

——. *Mother Teresa of Calcutta.* New York: Marvel Comics, 1984.

Ghezzi, Bert. "Mother Teresa's Contemplative Brothers." *Catholic Digest,* September 1986, p. l.

Gjergji, Lush. *Mother Teresa, Her Life, Her Works.* New York: New York City Press, 1991.

Gonzalez-Balado, Jose Luis. *Mother Teresa, Always the Poor.* Liguori, Mo.: Liguori, 1980.

———. *Stories of Mother Teresa, Her Smile and Her Words.* Liguori, Mo.: Liguori, 1983.

Goodwin, Jan. "A Week with Mother Teresa," *Ladies Home Journal,* May 1984.

Gorree, Georges and Jean Barbier. *Love Without Boundaries, Mother Teresa of Calcutta.* Huntington, Ind.: Our Sunday Visitor, 1974.

Hanley, Boniface. *Ten Christians,* Notre Dame, Ind.: Ave Maria, 1970.

Hendriz, Kathleen. "Mother Teresa's Brothers in L.A." *Catholic Digest,* July 1977.

Hess, Rev. Robert, S.C. *Passageway to Heaven, A Pilgrim's Diary.* Walls, Miss.: Sacred Heart League, 1987.

Hobden, Sheila. *Mother Teresa, People With a Purpose,* SCM Press Ltd., London, 1973.

"I Thirst: International Link Letter for Youth Coworkers of Mother Teresa," Malta.

"International Associations of Coworkers of Mother Teresa Newsletter," March 1983, Number 45.

Kaufman, Michael. "People...Mother Teresa." *San Francisco Chronicle,* December 10, 1979.

Kennedy, Terry. "Brother Anthony Joins Mother Teresa." *Catholic Digest,* August 1986, p. 47.

Kolodiejchuk, Brian. *Jesus Is My All in All: A Novena to Blessed Teresa of Calcutta.* San Diego: The Knights of Columbus, 2004.

Lee, Betsy. *Mother Teresa, Caring for All God's Children.* Minneapolis, Minn.: Dillon Press, 1981.

Le Joly, Edward. *Servant of Love, Mother Teresa and Her Missionaries of Charity.* San Francisco: Harper & Row, 1977.

———. *Mother Teresa: A Woman in Love.* Notre Dame, Ind.: Ave Maria, 1993.

———. *Mother Teresa of Calcutta, a Biography.* Minneapolis: Dillon, 1981.

Long, John C. "The Hands of Mother Teresa." *Catholic Digest,* October 1982, p. 24.

Marchand, Roger. *Mother Teresa of Calcutta, Her Life and Her Work.* Liguori, Mo.: Liguori, 1982.

McBride, Alfred. "Little Sisters Exalt Human Value." *The Catholic Times,* July 1, 1983, p. 9.

McGovern, James. *To Give the Love of Christ.* Mahwah, N.J.: Paulist, 1978.

Mohan, Claire Jordan. *Mother Teresa's Someday.* Worchester, Penn.: Young Sparrow, 1989.

"Mother Teresa of Calcutta." Press pack at the opening of Missionaries of Charity House in San Francisco, 1982.

"Mother Teresa Speaking at National Presbyterian Church." Washington, D.C.: Coworkers of Mother Teresa in America, 1974.

"Mother Teresa Speaking at National Shrine of the Immaculate Conception in Washington, D.C., and at Notre Dame University." Washington, D.C.: Coworkers of Mother Teresa in America, 1975.

Mother Teresa. "A Christmas Message," *Good Housekeeping*, December 1983, p. 145.

——. *A Gift for God, Prayers and Meditations*, New York: Harper and Row, 1975.

——. *Heart of Joy*. Ann Arbor, Mich.: Servant, 1987.

——. *Jesus, The Word to be Spoken*. Angelo Devanda Scolozzi, ed. Ann Arbor, Mich.: Servant, 1986.

——. "Joy," *Family Circle*, April 1, 1980, p. 61.

——. *Life in the Spirit, Reflections, Meditations and Prayers*. San Francisco: Harper & Row, 1983.

——. *Love: A Fruit Always in Season, Daily Meditations by Mother Teresa*. Dorothy S. Hunt, ed. San Francisco: Ignatius, 1987.

——. *Loving Jesus*. Jose Luis Gonzalez-Balado, ed. Ann Arbor, Mich.: Servant, 1991.

——. *My Life for the Poor*. New York: Ballantine, 1987.

——. *One Heart Full of Love.*, Jose Luis Gonzalez-Balado, ed. Ann Arbor, Mich.: Servant, 1991.

——. "Our Ministry to the Poor, God's Expectation for Us," Talk at the University of San Diego, 1988.

——. *Total Surrender*. Angelo Devananda Scolozzi, ed. Ann Arbor, Mich.: Servant, 1985.

——. "Woman and the Eucharist, 41st Eucharist Congress." Ann Arbor, Mich.: Congress Cassettes, 1976.

——. *Words to Love By*. Notre Dame, Ind.: Ave Maria, 1983.

"Mother Teresa, Indian Nun, Wins Nobel Peace Prize." *Los Angeles Times,* October 18, 1979.

Mother Teresa and Brother Roger of Taize. *Meditations on the Way of the Cross*, New York: Pilgrim, 1987.

Muggeridge, Malcolm. *Something Beautiful for God, Mother Teresa of Calcutta*, New York: Harper and Row, 1971.

"From Mother Teresa." Newsletter of Archdiocese of San Francisco, Spring 1982.

Petrie, Ann. "The World of Mother Teresa," Ann Petrie Productions, 1985.

Petrie, Ann and Jeanette. *Mother Teresa: The Legacy,* Petrie Productions, 2004.

Pogash, Carol. "In San Francisco, a Friend Sees Her as Christ Incarnate," *San Francisco Examiner,* October 17, 1979, p. 22.

Popson, Martha. *That We Might Have Life,* New York: Doubleday, 1981.

Porter, David. *Mother Teresa, The Early Years*. Grand Rapids, Mich.: William B. Eerdmans, 1986.

Prial, Frank. "Calcutta Nun Awarded Nobel Peace Prizes." *New York Times,* October 18, 1979.

Rae, Daphne. *Love Until it Hurts.* San Francisco: Harper and Row, 1981.

Reed, Edward, ed. *Pacem in Terris.* New York: Pocket, 1965.

Rodriquez, Robert D. "St. Therese, the Little Way and Mary." *Catholic Digest,* November 1982, p. 61.

Scolozzi, Brother Angelo Devananda. *Mother Teresa, Contemplative in the Heart of the World.* Ann Arbor, Mich.: Servant, 1986.

Sebba, Anne. *Mother Teresa.* London: Franklin Watts, 1982.

Serrou, Robert. *Teresa of Calcutta.* New York: McGraw Hill, 1980.

Spink, Kathryn. *I Need Souls Like You.* San Francisco: Harper and Row, 1984.

——. *The Miracle of Love.* San Francisco: Harper and Row, 1981.

——. *Mother Teresa: A Complete Authorized Biography,* San Francisco: HarperSanFrancisco, 1997.

Srinivasa, Murthy B. *Mother Teresa and India,* Long Beach, Calif.: Long Beach, 1983.

Sroka, Bill. "Mother Teresa's India," *Catholic Digest,* October 1980.

Suarez, Federico. *Our Lady, the Virgin.* Dublin, Ireland: Scepter, 1968.

Teresa of Avila. *The Autobiography of St. Teresa of Avila.* London: Doubleday, 1984.

Thérèse of Lisieux, *The Autobiography of a Soul,* John Beevers, trans. Garden City, N.Y.: Doubleday, 1957.

Tanghe, Orner. *For the Least of My Brothers: The Spirituality of Mother Teresa and Catherine Doherty.* Jean MacDonald, trans. New York: Alba House, 1989.

Tower, Courtney. "Mother Teresa's Work of Grace," *Reader's Digest Special Feature,* January, 1988, p. 285.

Vardey, Lucinda. *Mother Teresa: A Simple Path.* New York: Ballantine, 1995.

Ward, Barbara. *World Poverty: Can It Be Solved?* Chicago: Franciscan Herald, 1966.

Watson, Jeanene D. *Teresa of Calcutta, Serving the Poorest of the Poor.* Milford, Ill.: Mott Media, 1984.